AI

Social Work
and
Child Sexual Abuse

Social Work
and
Child Sexual Abuse

Jon R. Conte
David A. Shore
Co-Editors

Journal of Social Work & Human Sexuality
Volume 1, Numbers 1/2

The Haworth Press
New York

The Haworth Press, Inc., 28 East 22 Street, New York, NY 10010.

Library of Congress Cataloging in Publication Data
Main entry under title:

Social work and child sexual abuse.

(Journal of social work & human sexuality ; v. 1, no. 1/2)
Includes bibliographies.
Contents: Sexual abuse of children : enduring issues for social work / Jon R. Conte — Child sexual abuse in historical perspective / LeRoy G. Schultz — Social work and sexual oppression of youth / Harvey L. Gochros — [etc.]
1. Child molesting—Addresses, essays, lectures. 2. Child abuse—Services—Addresses, essays, lectures. 3. Social work with children—Addresses, essays, lectures. I. Conte, Jon R. II. Shore, David A. III. Series.
HQ71.S67 1982   362.7'044   82-11952
ISBN 0-917724-98-4

Social Work
and
Child Sexual Abuse

Journal of Social Work & Human Sexuality
Volume 1, Numbers 1/2

Contents

ABOUT THE EDITORS

Jon R. Conte is an Assistant Professor at the School of Social Service Administration, University of Chicago. A social work educator and researcher, he has lectured on the topic of sexual abuse of children at national and international meetings. His publications cover various aspects of social work, families, and sexual abuse. Dr. Conte has served as a consultant to social service, medical and criminal justice agencies. He is currently the Principal Investigator of a study funded by the National Institute of Mental Health to study the impact of sexual abuse on children.

David A. Shore is program manager for psychiatry, Department of Education, Joint Commission on Accreditation of Hospitals. He is the former director of a private child welfare agency in Chicago. Certified by the American Association of Sex Educators, Counselors and Therapists in all three categories, Mr. Shore is the founding editor of the *Journal of Social Work & Human Sexuality* and is on the editorial board of numerous professional journals. He has provided consultation and staff development programs for mental health and social service agencies, schools and residential facilities throughout the United States and abroad. Mr. Shore is the recipient of four consecutive grants from The Playboy Foundation to study various aspects of human sexuality. His most recent book is *Sexual Problems of Adolescents in Institutions*.

Contributors

Lucy Berliner, MSW
Social Worker
Sexual Assault Center
Harborview Medical Center
Seattle, Washington

Josephine Bulkley, JD
Director, Child Sexual Abuse Project
National Legal Resources Center For
  Child Advocacy and Protection
American Bar Association
Young Lawyers Division
Washington, D.C.

Susan Meyers Chandler, PhD
School of Social Work
University of Hawaii
Honolulu, Hawaii

Jon R. Conte, PhD
The University of Chicago
The School of Social Service
  Administration
Chicago, Illinois

Thomas S. Gary, MEd
Consultant
Sex Offender Program
Connecticut Correctional Institution
Somers, Connecticut

Harvey L. Gochros, DSW
School of Social Work
University of Hawaii
Honolulu, Hawaii

A. Nicholas Groth, PhD
Director
Sex Offender Program
Connecticut Correctional Institution
Somers, Connecticut

William F. Hobson, MS
Mental Hygiene Unit
Connecticut Correctional Institution
Somers, Connecticut

Kee MacFarlane, MSW
Child Sexual Abuse Specialist
National Center on Child Abuse and
  Neglect

United States Children's Bureau
Department of Health and Human
  Services
Washington, D.C.

Carl M. Rogers, PhD
Director of Research and Evaluation,
  and Associate Director,
Child Protection Center Special
  Unit
Children's Hospital and National
  Medical Center
Washington, D.C.

LeRoy G. Schultz, MSW
School of Social Work
West Virginia University
Morgantown, West Virginia

Suzanne M. Sgroi, MD
Co-Director, Saint Joseph College
  Institute For the Treatment
  and Control of Child Sexual
  Abuse
West Hartford, Connecticut

Doris Stevens, ACSW
Director, Sexual Assault Center
Harborview Medical Center
Seattle, Washington

David A. Shore, ACSW
Program Manager
Department of Education-Psychiatry
Joint Commission on Accreditation of
  Hospitals
Chicago, Illinois, and
Editor, *Journal of Social Work and
  Human Sexuality*

Joseph Zefran, MSW, Researcher,
  Harry F. Riley, MSW, Supervisor
  William O. Andersen, MA, Jeanne
  H. Curtis, MEd., Linda M. Jackson,
  MSW, Paul H. Kelly, MA, Ellen T.
  McGury, MA, and Mary K. Suriano,
  MSW, Probation Officers,
Special Services Unit
Juvenile Court of Cook County
Chicago, Illinois

For our parents

William and Suzanne Conte
and
Milton and Ruth Shore

FOREWORD

Given the current plethora of journals, it appears a rite of passage of every founding editor to justify the existence of yet another periodical. Fortunately, my task is simplified by the observations of such eminent researchers as Alfred Kinsey and William Masters. Kinsey (1948) indicated that social workers were involved in dealing with their clients' sexual problems even more often than were physicians. This finding was in keeping with that of William Masters (1970), who determined that 75 percent of all sexual problems for which help was sought in this country were treated by members of four professions other than medicine and that social work was one of these professions. Despite the clear relationship between issues of human sexuality and family planning and the tasks and functions of social workers and social service delivery systems, the social work literature and the sexuality periodicals have historically had sexual blinders when it came to the publication of articles pertaining to human sexuality and social work populations and concerns. Or, perhaps such manuscripts were simply never submitted or solicited? Remarkably, it was not until 1970 that Gochros wrote the first article in a social work journal calling for the inclusion of material on human sexuality in the social work curriculum. In 1977 the *Encyclopedia of Social Work* devoted a major article to human sexuality. Similarly, schools of social work were slow to recognize the need for training in sex-related issues. More recently, they have realized the growing demands of the profession for specialized education. By 1975, 55 graduate schools of social work offered at least one specific course on human sexuality. In the past, social workers attempting to deal with sexual issues in their practice had to do so without the guidance of specific training and without the benefit of specific social work literature.

The introduction of a journal devoted exclusively to issues of social work and human sexuality is one step in bridging the gap between training and education and practice realities. It was born of necessity on three basic premises: (1) social workers are actively involved with clients and agencies who have or manifest sexual con-

xi

cerns; (2) there is currently a dearth of material specifically available to social workers on issues of human sexuality; and, (3) there are sex-related issues and concerns with regard to social work populations and social service settings that are particularly idiosyncratic to the field of social work.

While van Gennep did not list the rationale for a new journal as a rite of passage along side birth, puberty, marriage and death, a statement of need and accountability is indeed appropriate. We have attempted to provide it for the *Journal of Social Work & Human Sexuality* in the hopes that it will in turn help you provide it to your clients.

As a social work journal, we will focus heavily on sex-related concerns of those special populations most often served by social workers and in social service settings, e.g., adolescents; the aging; ethnic minorities; the homosexually-oriented; the institutionalized; the medically ill; the mentally retarded; the physically handicapped; poor people; sexual victims; and other traditionally oppressed populations. With this as its charge, the *Journal* should be of interest to mental health and health-related professionals.

This first issue inaugurates not only a new journal, but also a series of special issues devoted to single themes. These special thematic editions will be co-published simultaneously as a text, while other issues will publish articles of a generic interest to social workers involved with the broad range of issues pertaining to human sexuality and family planning. Plans are well underway for special volumes for the following: homosexuality and social work and medical social work and human sexuality. Suggestions for other special issues are most welcome.

We hope you find the *Journal* as stimulating, informative, and helpful as its preparation has been for us.

David A. Shore
Editor

PREFACE

Estimates describing the numbers of children who are sexually abused each year vary considerably. A recent report indicates that as many as ten percent of all boys and twenty percent of all girls are the victims of sexual abuse (Finkelhor 1979). The secrecy which surrounds sexual use of children by adults may always make it impossible to determine exactly how many children are victimized. Nevertheless, it appears that large numbers of children have in common, situations in which they become the object of adult sexual abuse. As a group, social workers are becoming increasingly aware that regardless of the settings in which they practice—schools, hospitals, child welfare, social service, mental health agencies, or correctional facilities—they routinely come into contact with children who have been, are currently, or will be the victims of sexual abuse.

Sexual abuse is a multi-faceted problem, involving a number of professional groups. Because it is against the law, attorneys and law enforcement personnel become involved with both victims and offenders. The potential for or actual physical trauma or disease resulting from the abuse involves medical professionals. The deviant behaviors of adults who sexually victimize children and the psychosocial aftermath in children's lives may require social service and mental health professionals.

Social work with its dual interest in "person-changing" and "context-changing" interventions can and should play a significant role in responding to sexual abuse of children. Social workers are needed to insure that other professional groups provide the necessary services to child victims and their families and that these services are provided in a manner which does not further traumatize those who have been already abused. Social workers are also needed who can view the wide range of possible effects of being sexually abused in the child's psychological and social life and provide a range of crisis and clinical interventions designed to minimize the immediate and long term effects of such abuse. Social workers can also advocate for the creation of special programs for both child victims and the adult offenders who victimize them. The roles social workers may play in responding to a

xiii

problem of such magnitude and complexity is only limited by our imagination.

Our growing awareness of the magnitude of the problem of sexual abuse and the special roles social workers may play in addressing this problem, have served as catalysts for this volume. The contributions collected here represent the state of knowledge concerning sexual abuse of children. They include reviews of the historical context in which sexual abuse takes place, issues surrounding the professionals' responses to sexual abuse, alternative models of sexual abuse treatment programs, and practice knowledge developments. Contributors have also addressed a number of clinical issues including family treatment and social work treatment at a juvenile court, as well as the role of the courts and the heretofore unexplored problem of sexual abuse and sexual education in child-caring institutions.

As social workers become increasingly involved with sexually abused children and the adults who share and influence their lives, practice, research, and policy are likely to become increasingly knowledgeable. Our awareness of the problem is new, our commitment emerging, and skills developing. Therefore, this volume attempts to make statements about where we are as a profession at the same time as we venture forward on behalf of our children.

Jon R. Conte
David A. Shore

REFERENCE

Finkelhor, D. *Sexually Victimized Children*. New York: Free Press, 1979.

Social Work
and
Child Sexual Abuse

SEXUAL ABUSE OF CHILDREN: ENDURING ISSUES FOR SOCIAL WORK

Jon R. Conte, PhD

The topic of sexual abuse of children is receiving increasing attention in both lay and professional circles. Although for some time there has been a steady flow of articles in professional literature discussing sexual abuse, the last few years have witnessed an explosion of this literature. The articles in this volume provide a picture of the "state of the art" regarding sexual abuse of children. Although the organizing theme of this volume is *Social Work and Child Sexual Abuse,* it is an appropriate statement about the multifaceted nature of sexual abuse that articles have been contributed by attorneys, psychologists, sexologists, and physicians as well.

There may be no other subject matter which instills as heated an argument among mental health and social service personnel as that of sexual abuse of children. There are a variety of reasons for the frequent polemic nature of this argument, including the number of myths surrounding sexual abuse of children; the traditional disagreements among professionals of different theoretical models about etiology and treatment; a general lack of knowledge concerning most aspects of the problem; and the sensitivity of matters dealing with sexuality, especially deviant sexuality and children. While this article will not resolve these concerns, it is hoped that it will be successful in reviewing a number of enduring issues. The issues appear to be enduring in that they continually are raised and continue to affect the services provided sexually abused children and the adults who influence and share their lives. Some resolution of these issues, at least at the practice level, seems necessary if we are to move forward on behalf of sexually abused children.

What Is Sexual Abuse?

Some ambiguity surrounds what constitutes sexual abuse. Sexual abuse has been described as including a range of activities which involve the child's viewing sexual activity of adults (including exhibitionism, in which an adult exposes him/herself to the child(ren), accidentally or intentionally viewing adults having intercourse, and viewing sexually related materials such as movies or books). Sexual abuse also involves a range of sexual contact between adults and children from fondling, oral-genital contact, digital penetration, to intercourse. Sexual abuse also involves the use of children by adults in pornography. Sexual abuse is also sometimes thought of as sexual activity between same-age or near-age children and adolescents, as well as older adolescents and younger children.

The difficulty in viewing such a range of acts as sexual abuse is that such a view fails to discriminate between acts and consequently provides no guidelines to the social worker for clinical decision making. Such guidelines are necessary because not every act of "sexual abuse" represents the same potential risk to the victim. For example, the child who happens upon his parents having intercourse is not a victim of sexual activity in the same sense as the child who is coerced into having oral-genital contact with his/her uncle. Berliner and Stevens (this volume) provide an attempt to differentiate between types of sexual abuse when they offer the three categories of rape, child sexual abuse, and sexual exploitation. This typology and others which divide sexual abuse into categories by type of sexual contact, age of victim, relationship between child victim and adult offender are helpful in calling attention to the wide range of "acts" which make up sexual abuse. They are not particularly helpful in making practice decisions since so little is known about what variables (dynamics) are or are not associated with particular descriptive categories or what problems may be encountered in providing service to the various subtypes of sexual abuse. Intercourse with a father may or may not be more traumatizing than a child's being photographed without clothing for pornographic pictures. The child who becomes the victim of an exhibitionist may require more intensive social work interventions than the child who is victimized by an uncle who fondles her/him.

The issue in terms of what is sexual abuse seems to call upon the social worker to recognize a wide range of situations as *potentially abusing* and to remain open to individual children's reactions which may be exacerbated by other factors. Singling out one type of abuse as being of greater concern is premature.

Related to this issue of *what is sexual abuse* is the concern expressed by Gochros and Schultz in this volume; that adults, because of their own discomfort with the subject, often try to prevent children from experiencing and expressing their own sexuality. Although this view does not always fully distinguish between a child's sensuality and his/her sexuality, the injunction not to deny or "oppress" a normal part of a child's life seems an especially apt one for a profession whose goals are the "best interests of the child." Equally important is recognizing the fundamental difference between a child's right to express inherent sexuality/sensuality and the *sexual use* of a child by an adult. Same-age children involved in exploration of each other's sexual organs or sexual activity between same-age adolescents is fundamentally different than sexual contact between an adult and a child.

Discriminating between sexual (genital) contact and sensual (tactually pleasing) contact may not be as difficult in reality as it appears conceptually. The clear instances of sexual abuse would seem to include: intercourse, oral-genital contact, digital penetration, and the use of children in pornography. Other areas which involve accidental contact (when an adult is bathing a child or a child enters her/his parent's bedroom while they are sexually involved) or physical contact which may have a sensual aspect (rubbing a child's back) may or may not be abusive depending on a number of factors. These factors include: *developmental appropriateness* which directs attention to several issues including the similarity-dissimilarity in age between actors in the sexual situation and the degree to which the activity is a developmentally appropriate expression of sensuality/sexuality; and *intent* which, although apparently vague, directs attention toward whose needs and what types of needs are being satisfied by the contact. For example, is a parent rubbing a child's back a means of communicating warmth and affection with a secondary tactually pleasing quality or a means of relieving an adult's sexual sublimations? (See Rosenfeld [1977] for a helpful set of guidelines for establishing acceptable boundaries of sexual behavior in families.)

Intrafamily versus extrafamily abuse. A common belief among practitioners is that sexual abuse of children is a fundamentally different phenomenon when the offender is a family member versus when he is not a member of the child's family. In support of this view, literature is often cited which describes incestuous behavior as a collaborative dynamic between father, mother, and daughter (see pp. 6–8). The tenacity of this belief may in large part be responsible for the different professional stances taken with incestuous versus nonincestuous sexual abuse cases. These differences include a greater reluctance on the part of many social workers to support state intervention into family life in cases where the offender is a family member versus not a family member. These differences also may account for the tendency to value maintaining the family unit over removing the offender or child to insure the protection of the child. There is little data which inform questions about the similarities or differences in intrafamily versus extrafamily sexual abuse. However, there are a number of problems which raise some doubt about the validity of the assumption that they are different phenomena. While waiting for research data which will put to rest this ambiguity, these problems should be considered when thinking about the beliefs and assumptions upon which practice has been based.

To begin with, it is not clear why so much energy has gone into speculating about intrafamily sexual abuse (which usually means father/stepfather-daughter incest). Although there has been some discussion of other types of sexual abuse (see father-son incest [Dixon, Arnold, and Calestro, 1978]), the bulk of literature has focused on father-daughter incest, which is a small proportion of the total victim population. Data reported by Conte and Berliner (1981) on a sample of 583 sexually abused children indicates that 16 percent of the cases involved the father as the offender, an additional 15 percent involved stepfathers, 15 percent other relatives (grandfathers, uncles, brothers), 6 percent nonrelated parenting figures (e.g., mother's boyfriend), 8 percent involved a stranger, and 35 percent an acquaintance of the child or child's family (2 percent offenders listed as others).

One wonders whether the interest in father-daughter incest over other kinds of sexual abuse of children reflects a salacious or theoretical bias of the professional rather than a substantive difference. Indeed, such a question leads one to ponder the extent to which theoretical biases about families established a priori in the minds of certain clinicians have predetermined the kinds of family dynamics, individual personalities, and developmental histories which subsequently have been reported in many incest cases. Since reports of incestuous families have been unaided by objective measurement or adequate control procedures, these questions cannot be put to rest at present.

There is some evidence to indicate that incestuous and nonincestuous child molesters share more in common than there is that separates them. A number of authors describe a similar type of person who commits sexual offenses against children. They are seen as dependent, inadequate individuals with early histories characterized by conflict, disruption, abandonment, abuse, and exploitation (see especially Groth et al., this volume, and also Swanson, 1968). Panton (1979) compared the MMPI profiles of incestuous offenders and nonincestuous child sex offenders and found common features, including feelings of insecurity, inadequacy in interpersonal relationships, dependency, and early family histories characterized by social isolation and family discord. The only significant difference was that the nonincestuous offenders functioned at a lower level of sexual maturity.

Part of the belief that intrafamily sexual abuse is different than extrafamily sexual abuse is the belief that incestuous fathers tend not to involve children outside of their family as sexual objects, and the incestuous behavior begins as husband-wife sexual contact terminates. Although representative data is lacking, there is evidence to suggest that the pattern is more complex than this. In fact, there is great variation in whether men have exclusive or multiple sexual relations with their daughters, other children outside the home, and their wives. For example, Joaiassen, Fantuzzo, and Rosen (1980) report on the case of a thirty-seven-year-old man who has pedophilic experiences during a time which he was also having sexual relations with his wife. Marshall (1979) reports on the case of a thirty-three-year-old male arrested for sexual relations with the thirteen-year-old daughter of a neighbor family and who continued having sexual intercourse with his wife (approximately three times a week). Although this offender never abused his own children, he abused approximately twenty-five young girls over a six-year period.

Data describing sexual offenders is varied and not clearly integrated: Swanson's early report (1968) on twenty-five sexual offenders indicates that 75 percent had adult sexual orientations and only about 20 percent had developed pedophilic interest in their own childhood or early adulthood. Some of these cases had turned to a child(ren) as a result of conflict with or loss of their usual source of sexual satisfaction, while in other cases their daughters had assumed the role of substitute wife generally, and still others seemed to be reacting to multiple stressful circumstances. Groth (1979) reports that 32 percent (N = 348) of offenders in his sample had reported sexual trauma in their formative years (27 percent of the assailants in these cases were adult women). Quinsey, Chaplin, and Carrigan (1979) indicate that incestuous child molesters show more appropriate sexual arousal preference than nonincestuous child molesters.

The only clear point of the preceding evidence is that sexual abuse of children is committed by a wide range of adults, largely but not exclusively adult men. As Berlin and Meinecke (1981) have suggested, there is little known about etiology of deviant sexual behavior. Although early life experiences are thought to contribute to its development, little is known about the etiology of erotic desires and fantasies. Organic pathologies (genetic, hormonal, or neurological) may be related (see also Groth, 1979). To date there is insufficient evidence to make a decision about whether the choice of the child sexual object (family member or not a family member) reflects a real difference in types of pathology or happenstance. What would seem more plausible is that in some cases sexual abuse of children is related to dynamics within the family, and in other cases it is not. Indeed, it is unlikely that all sexual abuse of children reflects a common psychopathology. There may be a wide range of "reasons" that adults sexually misuse children. Additional research is necessary to categorize cases of child sexual abuse into functional typologies which consider all possible variables before classification.

Etiology of Incest

Although a subtype of sexual abuse, the dynamics of intrafamily sexual abuse have received proportionately more attention in professional literature, and illustrate a number of the more important inadequacies in professional understanding about etiology generally. This section will briefly review some of the more popular views about the development of incest. Incest has been referred to as the "perverse triangle" in which an adult forms a cross-generational (e.g., father-daughter) coalition against the same-age peer (Rist, 1979). A commonly described dynamic finds the daughter assuming many of her mother's traditional domestic roles (e.g., cooking dinner, supervising younger siblings). Already poor marital relations deteriorate further until sexual relations between the father and mother completely cease as a result of some situational factor (mother has a new baby or temporarily is absent from the home). The father, who is unwilling to act out sexually outside of the family, turns sexually to the daughter who has already stepped into many of her mother's duties. Fear of family disintegration and abandonment motivates all three of the participants in a pathological system in which sexual abuse becomes a tension-reduction mechanism maintaining the integrity of the family (Lustig, Dresser, Spellman, and Murray, 1966; and Kaufman, Peck, and Tagiuri, 1954).

For the fathers, incest becomes a means of projecting the hostility felt toward their own mothers whom they preceive as abandoning them as children and for fulfilling through a liaison with their daughter the Oedipal liaison denied them as children (Lustig et al., 1966; Cavallin, 1966). Overpowering feelings of inadequacy, dependency, and anxiety become disguised as genital urges and directed toward those in the family least capable of retaliation (their daughters) as relief from the fear of abandonment (Gutheil and Avery, 1977). Previous old Oedipal strivings and hostility toward the father's mother become rekindled by relationships with a withdrawing and cold wife and are given unconscious expression through incest (Cavallin, 1966).

Most frequently, the incestuous mother is seen as the "cornerstone of the pathological family system" (Machotka, Pittman, and Flomenhaft, 1967; Weiner, 1964; Bastani and Kentsmith, 1980; and Brant and Tisza, 1977). These mothers are described as having poor relationships with their own mothers, whom they see as stern, demanding, controlling, cold, hostile, and rejecting (Kaufman et al., 1954). The mother singles out one of her daughters (usually the oldest) to psychologically replace the mother's own mother. The daughter is then indulged materially and expected to assume responsibility for meeting the mother's emotional needs and running much of the household. The mother then is able to displace her anger and hostility for her own mother (who abandoned her and was emotionally unavailable) on her mother substitute (her daughter) by pushing her into bed with the father (Kaufman et al., 1954). This also serves to relieve the mother of sexual pressure from the father (Gutheil and Avery, 1977; Machotka et al., 1967).

For the incest victim, the father becomes a weapon against her mother who is seen as cruel, unjust, and depriving and as a means of obtaining the attention from her father she is denied by her mother (Gutheil and Avery, 1977; Machotka et al., 1967; Rist, 1979).

There are a number of significant problems with this paradigm of etiology:

The vast majority of the preceding literature is based upon clinical observations of extremely small samples, unaided by objective measurement or procedures to control for biases. It is impossible to tell how valid observations are or in how many cases of sexual abuse specific observations may be found. Additionally, for every characteristic described in the literature, social workers can find cases which disconfirm the importance of that characteristic. For example, for every incest case in which a breakdown in marital relations (especially sexual relations) preceded the onset of sexual abuse, there is a case in which incest took place during the same time as the husband and wife were engaging in sexual relations. (Brownnell, Haynes, and Barlow 1977 present a case in which the husband fantasied about sexual relations with his daughter while engaged in sex with his wife.)

A second problem area with respect to etiology has to do with its inherent sexist frame of reference. A number of authors have taken a feminist perspective and attacked much of the work in this area. For example, Herman and Hirschman (1977) have suggested ". . .seduction of daughters is an abuse which is inherent in a father-dominated family system" (p. 741). Similarly, McIntyre (1981) questioned much of the knowledge about sexual abuse for failing to recognize the impact of "patriarchy and the influence of male dominance on virtually every sphere of thought and action" (p. 462) (see also Butler, 1980).

The feminist perspective can be applied in two ways to sexual abuse: one dealing with the general culture in which sexual abuse of children takes place and the other concerning professional responses to these children. While an understanding of the extent to which patriarchy and sexism pervades Western life might be important in identifying variables which potentially are related to sexual abuse, to date, the feministic perspective has not identified these variables. It has done little to help us understand why some men sexually abuse children and others do not. Nor can it account for why some women (approximately 5 percent of the offenders reported by Conte and Berliner, 1981) also sexually abuse children. This perspective may, in the future, especially if aided by research conducted from its frame of reference, tell us much about the etiology of sexual abuse and how to control it. To do so, however, the perspective is going to have to become considerably more refined and specific about ways in which sexist values and assumptions operate to account for sexual use of children. One approach might be to study men who do not sexually abuse children in spite of prevailing sexist cultural values (although the methodological problems are great in determining with accuracy that a sample of men do not in fact sexually abuse children). The problem here is not the validity of the feminist perspective but rather that it has not been developed in sufficient detail to help us understand sexual abuse of children.

What the feminist perspective has been particularly helpful in doing is calling attention to the sexist bias of much of the helping literature (see especially Stevens, 1980). These biases operate in a number of ways. First, as Stevens points out, social work theories about sexual abuse have tended (along with other helping professions) to make the victim or victim's mother responsible for the sexual abuse. To suggest that the mother's psychiatric picture is always the central dynamic in family incest and not the offender's (even though each may be equally pathological) cannot be justified on any grounds other than a sexual bias. Second, sexism is so ingrained and unconscious many professionals are not aware of the degree to which it affects their observations and assumptions about sexually abused children. Several examples illustrate this point.

- Weiss, Rogers, Darwin, and Dutton (1955) identify two types of victims: participant and accidental. The difference between the two categories is based *only* on the frequency of sexual activity. Indeed, the authors point out that in almost all cases of accidental victims the offender is a stranger. This view seems to hold that by definition when the offender is a family member the child has to have been an active and willing participant. Weiss and colleagues go on to describe the participant victims as "attractive" and "appealing." It is not clear why a child's physical appearance is an important variable nor why an adjective used to describe adult physical characteristics be applied to children.
- Revitch and Weiss (1962) indicate that it is their impression that often the child victim is seductive and aggressive and induces

the adult to commit the offense. This is a particularly interesting observation since they also indicate that "we rarely had the opportunity of examining the victim" (p. 74).

• Weiner (1964) gives as evidence for daughters' collusion in incest the frequency and duration of sexual activity and the lack of "protest" and "resistance" by the daughters. Such a view seems to ignore the power fathers exercise to obtain compliance and to maintain the secret.

• Brant and Tisza (1977) give an example of a child who is involved in the incest only because she was "playing at riding a horse while bounced upon her father's leg" (p. 85). Such a statement would not seem possible had not the authors a priori believed that children were responsible for their own sexual abuse and seems to ignore altogether the question of intent. Was the child's intent sexual or playful?

In the examples presented above, what seems to have taken place is that professional assumptions and values about sexual abuse predetermined the meaning which the authors gave to what they observed in actual cases of sexual abuse. In some of the examples, this predisposition served to make the victim responsible for what took place. In others, it pictured the child in terms which originate in a sexist view of the world (e.g., attractive, appealing). The meaning which is ascribed to behavior is largely determined by the professionals' conceptual/theoretical model. To the degree that professionals hold theories which implicitly, if not explicitly, blame the victim for the problem, or maintain that children initiate genital sexual activity, or act in ways which are *intended* to excite adults, then these will be seen in child behavior. However, these are not matters of fact. They are inferences given to observable behavior. Alternative inferences are possible. For example, sexually abused children occasionally exhibit stylized sexual behavior. Rather than viewing this as "seduction" it might equally be viewed as a means of tension reduction. This author once had case responsibility for a six-year-old girl who witnessed her father murder her mother by shooting the mother in the head. During the course of service to the child and the extended family which cared for her, it was revealed that the father, and at least one friend, had repeatedly molested the child. During play therapy sessions the child would periodically say to the therapist, "Let's do exercises," and pull her panties down around her ankles and "hump" the floor. This behavior was only exhibited when the male therapist and the child were alone in a playroom. (Upon subsequent transfer to a female worker, the behavior completely subsided.) Whether the behavior was "seductive" or a means of reducing tension caused by being alone in an isolated playroom with an adult male would seem to be a matter largely of how the adult observer viewed it.

Is It Harmful?

An answer to the question "Is sexual abuse harmful to the child?" is complicated by differing definitions of harmful. The issue is further clouded by a lack of controlled evidence describing the immediate and long-term effects of sexual abuse and variables accounting for differential effects of such abuse. There is also conflicting evidence in the literature. Studies describing the effects on children of sexual abuse are mixed. A number have noted no ill effects (Bender and Grugett, 1952; Lukianowicz, 1972; Yorukoglu and Kemph, 1966; Bender and Blau, 1937). Other studies have found a range of effects on child victims including depression, guilt, learning difficulties, sexual promiscuity, runaway behavior, and somatic complaints (Kaufman, Peck, and Tagiuri, 1954); physical complaints (e.g., stomachaches) and changes in behavior (Burgess, Groth, and McCausland, 1981); hysterical seizures (Goodwin, Simms, and Bergman, 1979; Gross, 1979).

In studies of adult women who had been victims as children, results are also mixed. A number of reports describe that child victims experience problems as adults: Benward and Densen-Gerber (1972) noted a correlation between antisocial behavior (drug abuse) and having been sexually abused. Tsai and Wagner (1978) found guilt over enjoying the sexual contact or related benefits, a sense of complicity ("I must have done something to make it happen"), negative self-images, depression, problems in interpersonal relationships (e.g., mistrust of men, inadequate social skills, compulsion to become involved with men similar to the offender), and sexual dysfunction (e.g., nonresponsive or lack of enjoyment). Herman and Hirschman (1977), in a study of fifteen psychotherapy clients who had been molested as children, noted a sense of distance, isolation, and negative self-images. Other studies report more mixed results. For example, Finkelhor (1980), in a study of 796 college undergraduates, found that students (men and women) who had been sexually abused as children (19 percent of the women and 9 percent of the men) had significantly lower sexual self-esteem.

From a practice perspective, the question of harm is difficult because any particular child may or may not reflect disturbance either prior to, during, or some time subsequent to disclosure of the abuse. Some children may exhibit marked changes in behavior with clear and dramatic disturbances. Other children may show no effect. Other children may internalize reactions to the abuse situation and show evidence of effects of abuse at some time later and even in adulthood.

This problem of the difficulty in describing the impact of sexual abuse in easily identifiable terms has led some to question whether there is anything harmful about sexual abuse. Questions as to whether the effects of sexual abuse outweigh the potential trauma of disclosure and intervention by justice or helping professionals have been poised. While this argument raises a complicated set of issues concerning the legal and ethical responsibility of not intervening, either independently or jointly by justice and helping personnel, our concern here is that it reflects an unnecessary distortion of the harm issue. There is no research evidence which suggests either that intervention is necessarily harmful or that any such purported harm is greater than the harm created by sexual abuse. Conceptually it is possible to imagine, and clinically we encounter cases of sexual abuse which have been so badly handled that in fact the intervention may have contributed additional trauma to the child and family. However, harm to the sexually abused child as a consequence of the sexual abuse and harm as a consequence of intervention constitutes separate issues (see discussion immediately following). Other bases than potential harm have been suggested for intervention. For example, Finkelhor (1979) suggests that the major issue justifying intervention is that children are inherently incapable of giving consent to sexual activity with adults. Children lack both the knowledge and the power to say "yes" or "no" which is implied in the ability to give informed consent. Conte (1979), referring to cases in which the offender is a family member, has suggested that intervention is justified since sexual abuse inherently threatens a child's right to "a family or at least to the support, nurturance, and other fundamental conditions which facilitate physical and psychological growth" (p. 11). Fersch (1980), taking a strong victim advocate view, has suggested that all sexual abuse be viewed as assault and dealt with accordingly.

Prosecution vs. Treatment

There is an ongoing debate among those who work with sexually abused children concerning the relative importance of involving the justice system in these cases. Indeed, as MacFarland and Bulkley (this volume) suggest, programs can be discriminated on the basis of how much involvement they desire with the justice system. (Although, as they point out, varying degrees of involvement are frequently not matters that treatment programs can fully control and are, rather, matters of local law.) Overall, debating the involvement of the justice system in these cases is not going to be a productive activity for social workers.

Sexual abuse is against the law in almost every state (for discussion of statutes, see Bulkley, 1981). It is unlikely that the state will lessen their interest in sexual abuse of children in the foreseeable future. While there is little evidence documenting the harmful effects of state intervention, it seems likely that insensitive handling of these cases may result in some trauma. From a victim's perspective, the process of justice system involvement may be potentially problematic (Melton, 1980; Conte and Berliner, 1981). The child may have to recount the history of the abuse a number of times to police, prosecuting attorneys, and in a courtroom under insensitive questioning from the defendant's attorney. The process may extend over a number of months and, depending on what happens to the child and her/his family as a result of the process, the child may feel a sense of guilt (e.g., in intrafamily cases, when there is loss of income resulting from removal of the offender). Trauma resulting from actual courtroom appearances seems unlikely, if data is indicative as reported by Rogers (this volume) that only 2 percent of children appear in court and Conte and Berliner (in press) that only 27 percent appeared in court. Indeed, Finkelhor (1981) reports that the degree of criminal justice system involvement varies greatly from state to state. However, on the average, only 31 percent of the nonfamily and 23 percent of the family cases involve court action.

While justice system involvement in these cases may be problematic, it may also have advantages in terms of the degree to which it insures that offenders will receive and complete treatment (Giarretto, 1978). While some have questioned the extent to which an offender may "voluntarily" accept treatment as a means of avoiding prosecution, from a victim's perspective such a device insures that the offender will be engaged in efforts to correct his problem. Data reported by Conte and Berliner (in press) on eighty-four offenders indicates that only 12 percent actually spent time in prison, and 13.5 percent were committed to a sexual psychopath treatment program. The remaining 75 percent remained in their home communities, of which 52 percent received counseling as a condition of probation. From a social work perspective, there seem to be several issues that need to be considered. Since justice system involvement is likely to continue to be an aspect of sexual abuse cases and to the extent that such involvement is or may constitute a source of traumatization for the sexually abused child, the child's family, and/or the offender, social work activities should be directed toward altering the way the system operates. A number of authors have discussed specific ways that the justice system may be altered to help rather than harm child clients (see, e.g., Conte and Berliner, in press; Melton, 1980). From the victim's point of view, these include: reducing the number of times that the child has to recount her/his story to justice system personnel; and training these personnel to be more effective and sensitive interviewers.

Little social work attention has been given to the possibility of traumatization by insensitive handling of sexual abuse cases by public agencies assigned the responsibility of child protection or by social work interventions themselves. With the move toward deprofessionalization, many undertrained or inappropriately trained individuals have been given the responsibility of investigating incidences of sexual abuse of children. There has been virtually no discussion of how these individuals handle such cases. Similarly, little attention has been paid to ways in which social work interventions have contributed to the traumatization of sexually abused children and their families. As professional awareness of the problem has increased, many practitioners have focused attention in their cases on sexual abuse. It is conceivable that such attention may be insensitively handled by applying unproven theoretical models to sexual abuse; by continuing to direct casework time to the sexual abuse long after the client is ready to allow the wounds to heal; or other ways, as yet unknown.

The potential to mishandle, either through ignorance, insensitivity, or error, lies with all professionals who deal with sexually abused children. Each of the major professional groups—justice, child protection, medical, and therapeutic—has a legitimate role to play in handling these cases. An evaluation of the process of such handling should identify areas which are potentially problematic.

Social workers can help child protection and justice procedures operate with an understanding of children's developmental capabilities; help make victims feel comfortable, less fearful; and be sensitive to the range of feelings which the child has about the experience with the justice system, the abuse itself, and the offender. Of equal importance is the degree to which social workers object to criminal handling of sexual offenders. In our role as advocates, efforts should be extended on behalf of this client group. Advocacy on behalf of specific offenders and offenders as a whole may be extended to create diversion programs through which offenders receive treatment in lieu of jail or prison time; criminal and civil justice handling of offenders can be made more sensitive and less traumatizing; and treatment programs can be established. The reluctance to view offenders as a client group on whose behalf social workers advocate is partly a function of the strong victim advocacy history of the profession and especially the child sexual assault treatment programs. Additionally, the mood of the culture generally has shifted toward a prosecution/punitive approach to handling child abusers. Now seems like a good time for the profession to reframe its protreatment arguments and to increase its efforts on victims of adult sexual abuse (children) and victims of their own historical, psychosocial, and sexual makeups (offenders).

Moving Forward

The issues reviewed in the preceding pages are not new to those who work with sexually abused children. In one format or another they are discussed at national meetings, among local service providers, or at case conferences. The fact that they are enduring suggests that our thinking about sexual victimization of youth has reached a plateau. Indeed, a quick review of the references for the articles in this volume indicates a high degree of similarity. The field appears ready for work which will expand our knowledge about sexual abuse and upon which practice innovations may be based. This article rests upon several assumptions concerning what range of activities will be necessary to move forward from this point.

We desperately need rigorous research on virtually every aspect of sexual abuse. In spite of the fact that it is almost obligatory in volumes of this kind to call for more social work research, the evidence presented throughout this volume seems to cry out for such endeavors. While there exist ample descriptive reports (e.g., presenting the ages of children who are sexually abused or the relationship of child victim to offender), there has been little controlled research which compares various subgroups of victims and/ or offenders on some set of variables. Nor has there been much research which employs actual measurement of the variables under consideration.

We need to look afresh at sexual abuse and consider the degree to which our theoretical frames of reference may have biased what we have seen. The phenomenon of sexual abuse is complex, including a wide range of acts, victims, offenders, and psychosocial contexts. It is not at all clear if current theoretical frames of reference are adequate for understanding these phenomena. Although they may be quite adequate, however, we will not know this until we have more carefully analyzed these theories, subjected them to empirical test, and determined the extent to which they accurately describe and explain the wide range of phenomena which is sexual abuse.

The key to movement forward on behalf of sexually abused children may lie in the time-honored perspective of social work. Social work has traditionally viewed "person changing" and "context changing" activities as inseparable. This perspective calls for continued efforts to provide services to sexually abused children and the adults who share and influence their lives. Social work researchers may well seek out those variables in the psychosocial context of victim-offender environment which account for the development and maintenance of sexual abuse. Practitioners may search for services which more effectively help to control adult deviant sexual behavior which victimizes children and also those services which offer the greatest possibility that the child victim will recover and not suffer future problems as a consequence of having been sexually abused.

Social work advocates may seek policy and programmatic changes which insure that society's responses to sexual abuse of children victimize neither the child victims, their families, nor the offenders. *The efforts of the profession may be strengthened if social workers form a common interest.* Much is to be gained if social workers who see themselves as child advocates join with those who see themselves as family advocates as well as those who see themselves as offender advocates. A common problem joins these various groups as do the dangers of Reagan-economics. In this age of the assault on social services, it seems important to put aside differences based on single-purpose advocacy perspectives or unvalidated theoretical models and search instead for commonalities. Until it is clear that one perspective, program model, or theoretical frame of reference is the correct and single one, the open search for similarities may serve well. Indeed, in the long run, progress against sexual abuse of children may require such a common effort.

REFERENCES

Bastani, J. B., & Kentsmith, D. Psychotherapy with wives of sexual deviants. *American Journal of Psychotherapy,* 1980, *24*(1), 20–25.
Bender, L., & Blau, A. The reactions of children to sexual relations with adults. *American Journal of Orthopsychiatry,* 1937, *7*(4), 500–518.
Bender, L., & Grugett, A. E. A followup report on children who have atypical sexual experience. *American Journal of Orthopsychiatry,* 1952, *22*(4), 825–837.
Benward, J., & Densen-Gerber, J. Incest as a causative factor in anti-social behavior: An exploratory study. *Contemporary Drug Problems,* 1979, *4*(3), 323–339.
Berlin, F. S., & Meinecke, C. F. Treatment of sex offenders with antiandrogenic medication: Conceptualization, review of treatment modalities, and preliminary findings. *American Journal of Psychiatry,* 1981 *138*(5), 601–607.
Brant, R. S. T., & Tisza, V. B. The sexually misused child. *American Journal of Orthopsychiatry,* 1977, *47*(1), 80–90.
Brownell, K. D., Hayes, S. C., & Barlow, D. H. Patterns of appropriate and deviant sexual arousal: The behavioral treatment of multiple sexual deviations. *Journal of Counseling and Clinical Psychology,* 1977, *45*(6), 1144–1155.
Bulkley, J. (ed.). *Child sexual abuse and the law.* Washington, D.C.: American Bar Association, National Legal Resource Center for Child Advocacy and Protection, 1981.
Burgess, A. W., Groth, A. N., & McCausland, M. P. Child sex initiation rings. *American Journal of Orthopsychiatry,* 1981, *51*(1), 110–119.
Butler, S. Incest: Whose reality, whose theory. *Aegis,* Summer/Autumn, 1980, 48–55.
Cavallin, H. Incestuous fathers: A clinical report. *American Journal of Psychiatry,* 1966, *122*(10), 1132–38.
Conte, J. R. A child welfare perspective on children's versus parents' rights in incestuous families. Paper presented at 88th Annual Convention, American Psychological Association, Montreal, 1980.
Conte, J. R., & Berliner, L. Sexual abuse of children: Implications for practice. *Social Casework,* 1981, *62*(10), 601–606.
Conte, J. R., & Berliner, L. Prosecution of the offender in cases of sexual assault against children. *Victimology: An International Journal,* in press.
Dixon, K. N., Arnold, L. E., & Calestro, K. Father-son incest: Underreported psychiatric problem? *American Journal of Psychiatry,* 1978, *135*(7), 835–838.
Fersch, E. A. *Psychology and psychiatry in courts and corrections.* New York: John Wiley and Sons, 1980.

Finkelhor, D. What's wrong with sex between adults and children? *American Journal of Orthopsychiatry,* 1979, *49*(4), 692–697.

Finkelhor, D. Long-term effects of childhood sexual victimization in a non-clinical sample. Unpublished paper available from author at Family Violence Research Program, University of New Hampshire, Durham, N.H., 1980.

Finkelhor, D. Removing the child-prosecuting the offender in cases of sexual abuse: Evidence from the national reporting system for child abuse and neglect. Unpublished paper available from the author at the Family Violence Research Program, University of New Hampshire, Durham, N.H., 1981.

Giarretto, H. Humanistic treatment of father-daughter incest. *Journal of Humanistic Psychology,* 1978, *18*(4), 59–76.

Goodwin, J., Simms, M., & Bergman, R. Hysterical seizures: A sequel to incest. *American Journal of Orthopsychiatry,* 1979, *49*(4), 698–703.

Gross, M. Incestuous rape. *American Journal of Orthopsychiatry,* 1979, *49*(4), 704–708.

Groth, A. N. Sexual trauma in the life histories of rapists and child molesters. *Victimology: An International Journal,* 1979, *4*(1), 10–16.

Groth, A. N., & Birnbaum, H. J. Adult sexual orientation and attraction to under age persons. *Archives of Sexual Behavior,* 1978, *7*(3), 175–181.

Gutheil, T. G., & Avery, N. C. Multiple overt incest as family defense against loss. *Family Process,* 1977, *16*(1), 105–116.

Herman, J., & Hirschman, L. Father-daughter incest. *Journal of Women in Culture and Society,* 1977, *2*(4), 735–756.

Josiassen, R. C., Fantuzzo, J., & Rosen, A. C. Treatment of pedophilia using multi-stage aversion therapy with social skills training. *Journal of Behavior Therapy and Experimental Psychiatry,* 1980, *11*(1), 55–61.

Kaufman, I., Peck, A. L., & Tagiuri, C. R. The family constellation and overt incestuous relations between father and daughter. *American Journal of Orthopsychiatry,* 1954, *24*(2), 266–279.

Lukianowicz, N. Incest I: Paternal incest. *British Journal of Psychiatry,* 1972, *120*, 301–313.

Lustig, N., Dresser, J. W., Spellman, S. W., & Murray, T. B. Incest: A family group survival pattern. *Archives of General Psychiatry,* 1966, *14*(1), 31–40.

Machotka, P., Pittman, F., & Flomenhaft, S. Incest as a family affair. *Family Process,* 1967, *6*(1), 98–116.

Marshall, W. I. Satiation therapy: A procedure for reducing deviant sexual arousal. *Journal of Applied Behavior Analysis,* 1979, *12*(3), 377–389.

Melton, G. B. Psychological issues in child victims' interaction with the legal system. Paper presented at the first World Congress of Victimology, Washington, D.C., August 1980, available from author at Institute of Law, Psychiatry and Public Policy, University of Virginia.

McIntyre, K. Role of mothers in father-daughter incest: A feminist analysis. *Social Work,* 1981, *26*(6), 462–467.

Panton, J. H. MMPI profile configurations associated with incestuous and non-incestuous child molesters. *Psychological Reports,* 1979, *45*(1), 335–338.

Quinsey, V. L., Chaplin, T. C., & Carrigan, W. F. Sexual preferences among incestuous and nonincestuous child molesters. *Behavior Therapy,* 1979, *10*, 562–565.

Revitch, E., & Weiss, R. G. The pedophilian offender. *Diseases of the Nervous System,* 1962, *23*(2), 73–78.

Rist, K. Incest: Theoretical and clinical views. *American Journal of Orthopsychiatry,* 1979, *49*(4), 630–691.

Rosenfeld, A. A. Sexual misuse and the family. *Victimology: An International Journal,* 1977, *2*(2), 226–235.

Stevens, D. Dynamics of victimization. Paper presented at National Association of
Social Workers 1st National Conference on Social Work Practice with Women,
Washington, D.C., September 1980, available from author at Sexual Assault
Center, Horborrien Medical Center, Seattle, Washington.

Swanson, D. W. Adult sexual abuse of children. *Diseases of the Nervous System,*
1968, *29*(10), 677–683.

Tsai, M., & Wagner, N. N. Therapy groups for women sexually molested as children.
Archives of Sexual Behavior, 1978, *7*(5), 417–426.

Tsai, M., Feldman-Summers, S., & Edgar, M. Childhood molestation: variables
related to differential impacts on psychosexual functioning in adult women. *Journal of Abnormal Psychology,* 1979, *88*(4), 407–417.

Weiner, I. B. On incest: A survey. *Excerpta Criminology,* 1964, *4*( ), 131–155.

Weiss, J., Rogers, E., Darwin, M. R., & Dutton, C. E. A study of girl sex victims.
Psychiatric Quarterly, 1955, *29*(1), 1–27.

Yorukoglu, A., & Kemph, J. P. Children not severely damaged by incest with a
parent. *Journal of American Academy of Child Psychiatry,* 1966, *5*(1), 111–124.

CHILD SEXUAL ABUSE IN HISTORICAL PERSPECTIVE

LeRoy G. Schultz, MSW

The history of childhood in Western societies makes for disheartening reading, but when combined with childhood sexual development over time, it becomes one of unadultered ugliness. The historical evolution of childhood and sexuality is characterized by superstition, unreasonable fears, folklore, fanacticism and medical sadism. The discovery of "childhood" and "adolescence" as distinct from adulthood were a late invention (DeMause, 1974). The protection of childrens' and adolescents' sexual integrity emerged slowly and incrementally over several hundred years in both criminal law and in protective social services. This short history will attempt to pull together significant bits of historical evidence from the past and weave them into a coarse framework. The reader is cautioned as to historical accuracy, due to the sparcity of evidence, unfilled time gaps and the need for synthesis stretching.

At Risk as Norm

The taboo against using children and adolescents as sexual objects is only a few hundred years old. In very early times the age distinctions between child, adolescent and adult were not strong, and life was short by today's standards. As early as 100 A.D. young males were circumcised to help reduce their potential sexual arousal (Gochros, 1977), while others were castrated in infancy to enhance their later sexual appeal as boy prostitutes (DeMause, 1974). The early large cities of Europe and the Mediterranean Sea countries permitted marriages between boys and adults, boy houses of prostitution, and rent-a-boy sexual services. In early Rome, upper-class boys wore distinctive necklaces lest their fathers engage in sexual behavior with them by mistake in public bathhouses. Petronias (455 A.D.) described his rape of a 7 year old girl with the aid of older women who held the girl down and applauded on successful vaginal entry. Masturbation of children was thought to hasten growth and strength and to help hasten sleep.

Menstruation signaled sexual readiness for the female, adult marriage to children was common, as was routinely having intercourse with, or in view of ones children. Sleeping arrangements were crude and simple with all sleeping near the fireplace. Only the invention of the chimney and central-heating later were to allow for childrens' separate bedrooms. In the late 1600s, moralists recommended separate beds and rooms for children (Hunt, 1970; Flaherty, 1972) but they did not architectually evolve for some 200 years later. The clergyman Dominic was one of the first to indicate an interest in children's sexual protection from parents and in 1405 A.D. he warned parents (the chief child sex abusers of the time) to avoid nudity in front of one's children because of its temptations (Bullough, 1976). The sexual interest in older children was common among the wealthy. For example, Cellini, the renowned sculptor and pupil of Michelangelo, was a child-molester. In 1440 A.D. Baron de Rais, the Protector of Joan of Arc, was put to death for the rape-murder of some 800 children (Lipton, 1970; Rugglero, 1975).

By the 1500s some need for child sexual protection emerged legislatively in England. A law was passed in 1548 protecting boys from forced sodomy, and in 1576, protecting girls under 10 years of age from forcible rape (Radzinowicz, 1948). The state as protector of children's sexual integrity surfaced in the 1500s as a secular interest. For example, laws were passed in Germany which punished boys under age 14 years arrested as customers of prostitutes (Boesch, 1900). The books by the famous educator Gerson in 1706 suggested that children should be trained to avoid sexual victimization and that it was the duty of parents to induce guilt and trauma if children were discovered in self-pleasuring (DeMause, 1974). In this same time period the prominent educator Pascal wrote advice to parents for the prevention of child sexual abuse (DeMause, 1977; Moll, 1913). He warned parents to supervise children at all times of the day and night, to never pamper them, to prohibit children's nudity near adults, to closely control servants spending time with children, and the general enforcement of sexual modesty everywhere. These simple rules may be the first concrete help parents received from any source in controlling themselves and their children in terms of sexual interaction. A few years later the first sexual censorship of children's literature commenced. Thus, children's sexual innocence, as defined by the upper middle classes, and their sexual naturalness were to be curbed, bridled, restricted, and supervised. Parents were instructed by "experts" to keep candles burning in children's sleeping areas so that they may be checked for self-pleasuring (Aries, 1962, 109). Servants and the clergy were instructed to refrain from developing close relationships to children for fear of its sexual potential. Teachers were told to refrain from corporal punishment that included beating the child's naked buttocks since it could produce sexual pleasure. Some children of the well-to-do class were given as many as 1000 enemas to remove "evil" from their bodies (De-Mause, 1975; Ferriani, 1901). During this time, children were to be considered potentially sexually dangerous and consequently, asexuality was to be enforced. These developments foretold of the coming attack on children's sexual integrity by a well meaning society.

For Their Own Good

By approximately 1850 the medicalization of children's sexuality assumed that all pediatric problems could be attributed to early sexual activity and a wholesale effort to curb such activity commenced (Foucault, 1980; Comfort, 1967; Haller, 1974; Donzelot, 1979). The remedies proposed reflected current medical thinking as based on little understanding of childhood sexual development and an assumption of a simple physical relationship between mind and body. Among the remedies (Haller, 1975; Shade, 1978; Aries, 1962; Demause, 1974; Moll, 1913; Willson, 1905; Indiana State Board of Health, 1910; Gledstone, 1886; Thomas, 1959; Blackwell, 1879; Meigs, 1857) recommended to families were: instruction to parents on dressing children in loose clothing, (boys were instructed to avoid wearing underwear) recommendations for the separation of boys and girls in toilets, or walking to school together, the avoidance of rich food and drink, the regularity of outdoor exercise, a daily intake of vegetable tonic, avoidance of boy-girl wrestling, or girls climbing ropes. Parents were instructed to give regular cold baths, to avoid riding over rough roads, to avoid whipping the buttocks of children, to avoid sexual talk at home or displays of parental affection, to prohibit children viewing animals in heat, not permitting children to see parents make arrangements for their sexual love-making, the construction of special bicycle seats for girls, and, to a lessor degree, force feeding of strengthening tinctures, and opium enemas. Children and adolescents were not just to be protected from adult sexual attack or use. All the little angels of chastity also harbored the devil of depravity. Once society sensed that children were sexual beings in some degree, a fact admitted to 300 years earlier, law, medicine and education came forward to morally police their sexual development. Sexual feelings in children were to be circumscribed by the term "sexual precocity," and were presumed to lead to a wide variety of pediatric illnesses, particularly if manifested by self-stimulation or masturbation (Newman, 1975; Engelhardt, 1974; Comfort, 1967; Spitz, 1953). The child was viewed as a simple undisciplined animal who needs protection from himself. Added to medical intimidation and fear mongering was the societal fear of loss of control of minors during the long period from puberty to marriage, with increasingly earlier age of menstruation (Laslett, 1977). If children matured late, then parental supremacy endured longer. The family was "Gods Reformatory" and a frenzy of socially enforced anti-masturbation programs commenced (Comfort, 1967). The fear was that masturbation in boys led to insanity, growth retardation, or early death, and in girls, that masturbation lead to precocious sexual development, promiscuity and nymphomania. The emergence of the idea of childhood based on weakness and a need to be protected suggested that society and parents deny that children had sexual needs. Masturbation control efforts and programs occured in two rough time phases. Phase one (1850–1900) marked the period of forced sexual underdevelopment via surgery and phase two (1875–1925) via physical/psychological constraints. Surgical procedures practiced upon children only, consisted of partial or complete removal of the clitoris (sometimes without anesthesia), slitting or infibulating the penis, cauterization of clitoris or penis, castration of extra sexual active boys and the cutting out of nerves of both sexes' genitalia. As late as 1936 a common American medical textbook recommended that masturbation be controlled by circumcision of children (Holt, 1936).

The use of various constraints for desexualizing children consisted of the encasing the child in canvas and splints, encasing in plaster of paris, blistering the genitalia with red mercury, terror therapy, and if all these failed, committing the child to a "masturbation sanatoria"

(Spitz, 1953; Barker-Benfield, 1976). Parents could purchase chastity belts or girdles made of leather and bone to prevent "touching." An iron spike-ring could be placed around the penis, or "child-proof" gloves could be placed on the hands. Other methods consisted of immersing the child's sex organs in ice water, dressing the child caught masturbating in uniforms that told the community about it, placing bells on childrens hands at night, strapping hands to bedside, child battery, and a wide variety of trauma induction methods. Mercifully, by the 1920s raping children's sex organs in these ways, came to a slow end as a cure for "early" sexual development.

American Sex Law Reform

America, with its inherited English sex law, attacked the problem of sexual abuse in two ways. The criminal law developed a floor of sexual protection for children from adults, based primarily on whether force was employed. Emphasis was on conviction of offenders with little attention paid to victims. The child's or adolescent's consent to sexual activity varied as a factor in crime from age 10 to 21 years depending on time and place (Schultz, 1980). Such laws criminalize forcible rape, incest, sodomy, prostitution and very recently, children in pornography (Gigeraff, 1968; Schultz, 1980). Secondly, the juvenile court was to enforce community concepts of morality for children primarily through the creation of status offenses. Child welfare services did not become national until the mid 1930s with the establishment of the state public welfare agency. In the mid 1970s, the child abuse media blitz, focusing national attention on the need for services, fostered the growth of the Child Protective Services in abuse, misuse and exploitation. These last two are relatively new concepts of sexual abuse and are open to definitional problems.

Between 1877 and 1885, a powerful coalition was formed calling itself the Social Purity Alliance, made up of feminists, social workers, the clergy and members of the Salvation Army, the Young Women's Christian Association and Women's Christian Temperance Union (Pivar, 1976; Schlossman, Wallich, 1978). The group mission was to preserve childhood sexual innocence, to rescue "sexual drunkards" and "fallen women." Their strategy was to force the age of sexual consent as high as possible for adolescent prostitutes and "normal" girls, thus overextending itself (Schultz, 1980;

Schlossman, Wallich, 1978). By 1883 another group, the White Cross Society worked to teach boys sexual self-control, i.e., celibacy, through religion and certain feminist values (Pivar, 1976). As Gorham states, "feminists tended to share the same feelings of anxiety over youthful female sexuality as other members of the middle-class. Although they felt obliged to redress the sexual wrongs done to working class girls by men of a superior class, they registered the same repugnance toward incorrigible girls as they had earlier toward unrepentant prostitutes. For them, as well as for more repressive moralists, the desire to protect young girls thinly masked coercive impulses to control their voluntary sexual responses and to impose a social code on them in keeping with the middle-class view of female adolescent dependency" (Walkowitz, 1980, 127). The effect of the new age-of-consent law was to give police, courts and social welfare agencies far greater jurisdiction over children and the poor.

In historical summary, to be sexually vulnerable in a moral vacuum in earlier history was replaced, over time, by a societally sanctioned effort to control for sexual precociousness or independence, while a set of protections against child sexual abuse emerged.

Social Work Roles

The state came to reflect in its laws controlling sexual expression, the most powerful groups' ideas of children and adolescence, and this took the form of limiting parental options in certain areas of family life. Controlling the sexual lives of family and children in certain ways were reflected in laws protecting children from sexual abuse by adults (criminal law and protective service law) and to retard sexual emancipation of children (status offenses in Juvenile Court) until age 16. The first recognized social welfare agency dealing with sexual abuse and children's "immoral" behavior, was established in New York in 1874, (Ross, 1980; Jenkins, 1905; Jenkins, 1906) with legal authorization to remove children from parents because of sexual abuse or immoral conduct. The organization's direction was clear from the start. Of its first 932 published cases, some 795 dealt with children's immoral conduct, i.e., sexual behavior, the rest with adult abuse (Ross, 1980). While SPCC tried to be humanitarian, it clearly discriminated against the poor, through middle class socialization tactics, and tried to eradicate cultural diversity among immigrants. Later, this middle-class bias in attitudes of child rearing was to characterize the Juvenile Court movement as well. The early profession devoted much time to solving the problems of adolescent prostitution, premarital pregnancy and venereal disease, and in promoting an anti-sexual attitude among minors (Carstens, 1921; Wilson, 1933; Wessel, 1947; Little, 1944; Edholm, 1907). While the early laws and social welfare programs were designed to protect females from entering commercial sex markets, the new laws were worded in such a way as to restrict sexual growth and activity of normal girls and boys up to age 21 years, "for their own good." For example, the New York Juvenile Code authorized state intervention for girls "in danger of becoming morally depraved" (Worthington, Topping, 1921, 283). The newly emerging profession of social work was uncertain as to whether the thrust of its efforts should be to integrate minors into adult society, including the sexual, or to preserve them from it until a certain age. One consequence of the preservation theme was a continuation of the romantic-innocence concept that inferred that minors were fearful of being involved in adult sexual activity, or adult-like sexual activity.

In the early years of the profession, social work's intervention in the problems of unwed parenthood, family planning and sex education were poorly accepted by the public. Social welfare institutions and services moved from protecting girls from a harsh society to protecting society from sexually active girls (Walkowitz, 1980; Schlossman, Wallich, 1978). This social movement also resulted in the creating of a new crime for boys called "statutory rape," and the criminalizing of girls voluntary sexual lovemaking in the status offense of "sexual incorrigibility" (Conners, 1979; Schultz, 1980; Greenfield, 1978). Both of these new laws forced social work into policing the sexual lives of adolescents and enforcing carnal apathy as the norm. Sexual generosity in minors was reprehensible if sold and incomprehensible if it was spontaneous.

The period 1900–1930 witnessed a union of moral reform, individualism, psychoanalysis and child saving programs in the strongly emerging profession of social work. The profession moved from a concern with punishment of offenders to rehabilitating victims and offenders and from private child rescue to public protective services.

Each large urban area swelled by immigration and migration, attempted to clean up on commercial sexuality (vice) by establishing so called Morals Courts (Worthington, Topping, 1921). These courts and their social control arms, attempting to curb "white slavery" or adolescent prostitution, passed law and policy that overextended itself and ended up intruding into the sexual expression of "normal" girls and boys. The purity reformers turned to the profession of social work to carry on with their philosophy and program of forced sexual socialization and repression for adolescents, while developing interventions for sexually abused children. Social works unity with the mental health movement induced a shift from viewing certain sexual expression as sin or immoral to the clinical labelling of such activity as "abnormality," "perversion" or "deviancy," thus continuing the medicalizing of sexuality. This labelling process helped shape both diagnosis and intervention from a medical model, for both actors in any sexual event. Since children were presumed to be innocent and consentless, sexual acts with them were automatically "traumatic."

The problem of the sexual abuse of children remained somewhat dormant after the "Morals Court" movement in the 1920s, up to the late 1940s and 1950s when pediatricians and radiologists rediscovered the "battered child syndrome." Since child abuse also included sexual abuse it wasn't long before a media campaign and much professional attention brought resources to bear on the problem. A political movement that swelled in the 1970s characterized by equality for children coupled with a strong anti-violence spirit gave rise to the passage of the 1974 Child Abuse Prevention and Treatment Act. Following soon were forced reporting laws for professionals dealing with abused children, with criminal and civil penalties for failure to report. The 1974 Act allowed federal resources, that states did not have or would not provide, for research, inservice training, and treating the problem of sexual abuse, capping a hundred year struggle for child protection.

The Future

Including sexual abuse or misuse within the definition of physical child abuse may prove to be an unfortunate historical alliance. It wrongly conveys a victim-offender dichotomy that does not always hold in sexual interactions, it wrongly conveys physical damage which is true in only 5%—10% of child sex-abuse, (Gagnon, 1965) it does not deal with voluntary consenting reciprocal sexual activities that may be non-damaging, it does not acknowledge that children and adolescents are sexual beings and that sexual expression is a minor's right if it does not risk pregnancy. Definitions of "sexual abuse" are dangerously vague and make clear professional intervention unlikely except in the obvious case situations. The very labelling and intervention in child/adolescent/adult sexual interaction may themselves be victimogenic or traumatogenic (Schultz, 1980 b). While both psychiatrists and social workers have criticized law enforcement and the law profession for inducing legal process trauma, they have not critically examined their own interventions for possible victimogenisus, traumatogenisus or iatrogenisus.

Traumatogenisus and iatrogenisus have not been seriously examined by the helping professions. They remain the "Legionnaires Disease" of the helping professions (Chapman, 1964; Torry, 1977). In the face of trauma assumption, the difficulty for some child victims centers on forcing them to take a short lived act in the child's mind, with few permanent consequences, and to enlarge it all out of proportion, forcing the child to reorient his ideas to the confused adult interpretation of the event. Since we all are expected to react severely to child-adult sexual encounters, such a reaction is bound to insure the *unlikelihood* of victims escaping the difficulties produced by the definition and interpretation. Needed are criteria to assist professionals on deciding the appropriateness of intervention or non-intervention. Early learning that occurs in sexual interaction, unless repeated over time, is no more than a link in the child's developmental chain. It is the "here and now" that has the powerful effect on behavior (Cass, Thomas, 1979; Clarke, Clarke, 1976; Courtois, 1979; Tsai et al., 1979).

It is no longer defensible to apply diagnostic and intervention models, appropriate to those victims who are truly victimized, to the large majority who apparently are not, thus placing some control on possible iatrogenisus. In order to fully evaluate victim interest it is necessary to weigh the consequences of intervention against those of non-intervention. Professionals advise parents on how to play down the sexual event to control for negative victim impact, they have cautioned the legal profession against creating legal-process trauma. It would be a short step for all professionals to do the same. Becoming a victim is a process, not just a status, a process we should understand before drawing conclusions about the actors in a sexual event. The manner in which we orchestrate the victim process may change victim impact. Intervention should not simply confirm victim-stereotypes. Janeway states, "The Power to define guarantees that the stereotypes themselves are created by the powerful and reflect only their view of life" (Janeway, 1980, p. 14). The power to define sexual abuse is not simply descriptive, but also prescriptive. All interventions should be evaluated not on the good they might do, but rather on the basis of the harm they might do; the standard for all child care interventions. Uncritical enthusiasm for intervention may compound the harm or waste time and this important aspect has not been brought to critical self-consciousness (Lalley, 1980).

Some new attitudes and ideas are now emerging that foretell of a change in professional and public images of "sexual abuse" which may impact definition of abuse, justified state intervention and treatment methods. Protection of "what" and protection from "what" await a clear functional answer. There are plenty of standards but no realistic definitions of sexual abuse. State intervention into family privacy must be justified in a democracy and this will be difficult in a poly-ethnic, multi-valued, and melting pot tomorrow. Some of these are, a sexual bill of rights for children and family members (Farson, 1977; Wells, 1976; Brongersma, 1980), sibling sexual activity that is positive (Finkelhor, 1980; Arnow, 1977), boy-man sexual activities that may be either constructive, nurturing or neutral, or adult-child incest activity that may be non-damaging (Farrell, 1981; Ramey, 1975; Ramey, 1980; Schultz, 1980(c); Bernard, 1979; Ingram, 1979).

No area of childhood/adolescent development and family relationship is more confusing then in the situation of incest. At present, no data exist that can reasonably guide societal or professional intervention in incest with any degree of certainty (Katz, Mazur, 1979). Tomorrow's findings, as "victims" come out of the closet we have put them into, may force us to reevaluate many sexual aspects of family life, and individual freedom for both child/adolescent and adult, which are based on myth, naivete, conventional wisdom and poor research recidivism (Winn, 1981; Lee, 1980; Bernard, 1975).

A Research Agenda for the Future

A strong research focus on child sexual victimization is mandatory and a priority. Sufficient resources must be made available to both research and victim and to fund intervention services at the same time. Ultimately, research findings should inform interventions, and money should be provided for this transfer. Such research results will shape the history of attitudes and interventions in the future. Some important issues for research to address are:

1. Sexual abuse should be divorced from physical abuse, in treatment, policy, and research. Sexual interactions are rarely physically damaging. All children are sexual beings from birth, and all children will mature to view sexual activities as normal, healthy, and worth striving for in themselves and others. Claiming that sexual activity between persons holding different amounts of power as always motivated by the need to dominate, humiliate, or over-power, as in forcible rape, does not adequately cover all the reasons for adult-child sexual activity and at some point is counter productive.

2. Law enforcement, mental health, and social welfare could be substantially helped by the development of a working definition of child sexual abuse that reflects the real world of children and adolescents, sexuality, and the new fields of victimology, feminism, and children's rights.

3. Research is needed on why so many families are not incestogenic, or, on why so many adults are not child sexual abusers. Our obsession with pathology and deviance may have obscured the one area offering the best preventive potential.

4. Research must be conducted on non-traumatized minors involved with adults and siblings in sexual activities. The results of such research may clear up much confusion and produce ideas for prevention, both primary, secondary, and tertiary. Are there sexual "crimes" without victims? Is the victim/offender dichotomy always appropriate?

5. Research is required to determine what interventions are appropriate in relation to type of sexual and family situation. Intervention, affected by victim's social class, ethnic group, age, consent issues, emerging life styles, and sexual and privacy rights has not appeared in the professional literature. At present, professionals have two choices. They may continue to treat all victims in the same way in the hope of helping a few and either wasting resources on, or damaging the rest, or they may counsel according to their own experiential knowledge of victim-situation differences with little research to guide them.

6. Some of the confusion surrounding the problems of sexual abuse within families might be controlled by the development

of a "sexual bill of rights" for all family members. Why must families serve only public ends and have only public duties? Why is family intimacy established only on society's terms?
7. Education programs (sex education, crime-prevention courses, etc., for young persons; and criminology, victimology, psychology, social work, nursing, psychiatry, for professionals) should acquaint the student, early, with an accurate, truthful conception of child sexual victimization and its multipotential aftermath. Efforts should be made to de-myth popular misconceptions regarding trauma, trauma-genisus, stressing pre-victim strengths and how the label "victim" has a negative pull on self-esteem. Prevention should start with stemming the tide of victim stereotyping and fatalism-hustling for the next generation.

Future generations of social workers may find it strange that child neglect definitions willfully exclude the concept of sexual neglect. Laws restricting voluntary sexual activity end up as criminal schemes against the full development of adolescence or free choice. In all historical periods children have served adult ends. As Rodgers stated, "In fashioning children for the society that adults envisioned, the child shapers cut off children in important ways from the society that adults made" (Rodgers, 1980, p. 364). The future should include reasonable protection of children's sexual integrity, flexible enough to reflect a variety of life-styles, social classes, ethnic groups and concepts of harmless sexual expression, without the destruction of the human potential for sexual love by repression in childhood and adolescence. A more reasonable, clear, operational and justified set of child/adolescent protections, and a more democratic distribution of sexual rights for minors awaits the future.

REFERENCES

Aries, P., *Centuries of Childhood,* New York: Vantage Press, 1962.
Arnow, P., An Interview with D. W. Pomeroy, *Multi-Media Resource Center Guide,* 1977, 2(4–5), 52–53.
Barker-Benfield, G., *Horrors of the Half Known Life,* New York: Harper and Row, 1976.
Bernard, F., Inquiry Among a Group of Pedophiles, *Journal of Sex Research,* 1975, 11, 242–255.
Bernard, F., Pedophilia: Consequences for the Child, in M. Cook, & G. Wilson, (eds.) *Love and Attraction.* New York: Pergamon Press, 1979.

Blackwell, E., *Counsel to Parents on the Moral Education of their Children*. New York: Brentanos Literary Emporium, 1879.
Brongersma, E. The Meaning of Indecency with Respect to Offenses Involving Children. *British Journal of Criminality*, 1980, 20, 320–25.
Bullough, V., *Sexual Varience in Society and History*. New York: Wiley and Sons, 1976.
Carstens, C., The Development of Social Welfare for Child Protection. *Annals of the American Academy of Political and Social Science*, 1921, 26, 36–41.
Cass, L., and C. Thomas, *Childhood Pathology and Later Adjustment*. New Jersey: Wiley and Sons, 1979.
Chapman, A., Iatrogenic Problems in Therapy. *Psychiatry Digest*. 1964, 25, 20–24.
Clarke, A., and A. Clarke. *Early Experience: Myth and Evidence*. New York: Free Press, 1976.
Comfort, A. *The Anxiety Markers*. London: Nelson, 1967.
Conners, P., The California Statutory Rape Law: Violation of the Minors Right to Privacy. *University of California (Davis) Law Review*. 1979, 12, 332–49.
Courtois, C. The Incest Experience and Aftermath. *Victimology*, 1979, 4, 337–47.
DeMause, L. *The History of Childhood*. New York: Psychohistory Press, 1974.
Donselot, J. *The Policing of Families*. New York: Pantheon, 1979.
Edholm, D. *Traffic in Girls and Rescue Missions*. 1907.
Engelhardt, H. The Disease of Masturbation: Values and Concepts. *Bulletin of the History of Medicine*, 1974, 48, 234–48.
Farrell, W., The Last Taboo: The Complexity of Incest, in B. Mrazek, & C. Kempe, (eds.) *Sexually Abused Children and their Families*. New York: Garland, (in press), 1981.
Farson, R. *Birthrights*. New York: Macmillan, 1977.
Ferriani, A. *Delinquency: Precocious and Senile*, 1901.
Finkelhor, D. Sex Among Siblings. *Archives of Sexual Behavior*, 1980, 9, 171–94.
Flaherty, D. *Privacy in Colonial New England*. Charlottsville: University of Virginia Press, 1972.
Foucault, M. *The History of Sexuality*. New York: Vantage Books, 1980.
Gagnon, H. Female Victims of Sex Offenses. *Social Problems*, 1965, 13, 191.
Gerber, G. Ross, C. Zigler, E. (eds.) *Child Abuse*. New York: Oxford University Press, 1980.
Gigeraff, A. *Sexual Deviation and the Law*. Toronto: University of Toronto Press, 1968.
Gledstone, J. Save The Boys, *Philanthropist*, May:2, 1886.
Gochros, H. and Gochros, J. *The Sexually Oppressed*. New York: Association Press, 1977.
Gorham, D. Child Prostitution and the Idea of Childhood in Late Victorian England. *Victorian Studies*, 1978, 21 353–69.
Greenfield, M. Protecting Lolita. *Women's Law Journal*, 1978, 1, 1–26.
Haller, J. and Haller R. *The Physician and Sexuality in Victorian America*. Urbana: University of Illinois Press, 1974.
Holt, A. *Diseases of Infancy and Childhood*, 1936.
Hunt, D. *Parents and Children in History*. New York: Basic Books, 1970.
Indiana State Board of Health. *The Sexual Plagues with their Rapid Invasion of the American Home*. Indianapolis, 1910.
Ingram, M. The Participating Victim. in Mo. Cook, & G. Wilson (eds.). *Love and Attraction*. New York: Pergamon Press, 1979.
Janeway, E. *Power of the Weak*. New York: Knopf, 1980.
Jenkins, E. The New York Society for the Prevention of Cruelty to Children. *Annals of the American Academy of Political and Social Science*, 1905, 1, 774–777.

Jenkins, E. The New York Society for the Prevention of Cruelty to Children. *Annals of the American Academy of Political and Social Science.* 1908, 3, 492–94.

Katz, S., and Mazur M. *Understanding the Rape Victim.* New York: Wiley, 1979.

Lalley, T. Some Research Perspectives on Evaluation of Services to Victims, *Evaluation and Change, Special Issues on Services to Survivors,* 1980, 90–93.

Laslett, P. *Family Life and Illicit Love in Earlier Generations.* New York: Cambridge University Press, 1977.

Lee, J. The Politics of Child Sexuality, in *Childhood and Sexuality,* Quebec: Editions Etudes Vivantes, 1981.

Lipton, D. *The Faces of Crime and Genius.* New York: Barnes, 1970.

Little, R. Consultation Services for Girls with V.D. *The Family,* 1944, July, 14–19.

Meigs, C. *Women: Her Diseases and Remedies.* Philadelphia: Blanchard and Lea, 1859.

Moll, A. *The Sexual Life of the Child.* New York: Macmillan, 1913.

Newman, R. Masturbation, Madness and the Modern Concept of Childhood and Adolescence. *Journal of Social History,* 1975, 8, 6–7.

New York Society for the Prevention of Cruelty to Children. *Annual Reports,* 1–9, 1875–1884.

Pivar, D. *Purity Crusade.* Westport: Greenwood Press, 1976.

Radzinowicz, L. *History of English Criminal Law.* New York: Macmillan, Vol. I., 1948.

Ramey, J. Dealing with the Last Taboo, *SIECUS,* 1975, 7, 1–7.

Rodgers, D. Socializing Middle Class Children, *Journal of Social History,* 1980, 13, 354–67.

Rossman, G. *Sexual Experiences Between Men and Boys.* New York: Association Press, 1976.

Rugglero, C. Sexual Criminality in Early Renaissance, *Journal of Social History,* 1975, 8, 18–37.

Schlossman, S., and Wallach S. The Crime of Precocious Sexuality, *Harvard Educational Review,* 1978, 48, 65–94.

Schultz, L. *The Sexual Victimology of Youth.* Springfield, IL. Charles C. Thomas, 1980a.

Schultz, L. Victim-helpers as Hostages to Ideology, Unpublished paper, First World Congress on Victimology, Washington, D.C., August, 20–24, 1980b.

Schultz, L. Family Sexual Victimology, Unpublished paper, Family Sexuality Symposium, Minneapolis, MN, June 2, 1980c.

Shade, W. A Mental Passion: Female Sexuality in Victorian America, *International Journal of Women Studies,* 1978, 1, 13–29.

Spitz, R. Authority and Masturbation, *Yearbook of Psychoanalysis,* 1953, 9, 110–125.

Thomas, K. The Double Standard, *Journal of the History of Ideas.* 1959, 20, 156–174.

Tindall, R. The Male Adolescent Involved with a Pederast Becomes an Adult, *Journal of Homosexuality.* 1978, 4, 378–82.

Torry, C. Iatrogenic Anguish Caused by Psychiatry, *Psychology Today,* March 24, 1977.

Tsai, M., Feldman-Summers, S. & Edgar, M. Child Molestation, *Journal of Abnormal Psychology,* 1979, 88 (4) 407–17.

Walkowitz, J. The Politics of Prostitution, *Signs: Journal of Women in Culture and Society,* 1980a, 6, 127.

Walkowitz, J. *Prostitution and Victorian Society.* New York: Cambridge University Press, 1980b.

Wells, H. *Your Child's Right to Sex.* New York: Stein and Day, 1976.

Wessel, R. *A Casework Approach to Sex Delinquents.* Philadelphia, Pennsylvania. University School of Social Work, 1947.

Willson, R. *The American Boy and the Social Evil,* Philadelphia, 1905.

Wilson, O. *Fifty Years of Work with Girls, 1883-1933.* Alexandria: National Florence Crittenden Mission, 1933.

Winn, M. What Became of Childhood Innocence, *New York Times Magazine,* January, 25 (15-17, 44-46, 54-55, 58, 68), 1981.

Worthington, G., and Topping, R. *Specialized Courts Dealing with Sex Delinquency.* New York: Hitchcock, 1921.

SOCIAL WORK AND THE SEXUAL OPPRESSION OF YOUTH

Harvey L. Gochros, DSW

Social work practice has historically focused on reducing obstacles to human potential. Our profession has come to accept that sexuality is inextricably bound to the fulfillment of human potential. For most people, it is a major ingredient of social functioning. Indeed, social workers have long been involved in dealing with sex-related problems in virtually all practice settings. Such prestigious sexologists as Kinsey (1948) and Masters (1970a) have acknowledged that social work is one of the primary professions which works with sex-related problems.

There no longer seems to be much question as to whether social workers *should* be involved with sex-related problems; social workers *are* involved. The more pertinent questions today are: are social workers attending to the most appropriate sex-related problems in the context of our profession's purposes and values, are they attacking the most appropriate targets and are they effective in dealing with these problems?

This author has previously suggested that given the nature and values of our profession, the most legitimate targets for our interventions are those who contribute to sexual oppression. Furthermore, our prime clients are the sexually oppressed (Gochros 1973 and Gochros and Gochros 1976). The sexually oppressed is that sizable segment of our population who violate the reproductive bias in that their sexual expression cannot lead to socially approved pregnancies. For that fact alone their sexual rights and opportunities are limited by various sources of social control—often including the "helping" professions. The sexually oppressed include such populations as the aging, the disabled, the institutionalized, the homosexually oriented and, the subject of the present collection of articles—children.

Assuming we chose to expand the sexual choices and opportunities of these groups as well as dilute the various forms of restrictiveness, punitiveness, exploitation, abuse and other forms of oppression which they encounter, how do we proceed? The first step would seem to be to consider the nature of sexuality in its social context. If we do that, we become aware how sexual values change over time and how subjective an experience sexuality is. For example, let us review the changes in sexual knowledge and attitudes which have occurred over the last decade. We can then consider some current attitudes about the sexuality of youth and the roles social workers can play in minimizing their exploitation while at the same time increasing their sexual options.

Sexual Changes in the Last Decade

If any proof is needed that sexual attitudes are cyclical, one need look no further than the last decade. The decade began with the publication of Masters' and Johnson's celebrated *Human Sexual Inadequacy* (1970) proved to be a turning point in professional and lay perceptions of sexual behavior. A year earlier a different event also had a profound impact on the sexual attitudes of the following decade. When police raided the Stonewall, a gay bar in Greenwich Village, in an effort to harass the customers, they fought back. This confrontation—the first of its kind—marked the beginning of the modern gay liberation movement. Throughout the decade other groups—women, the aged, the disabled—pressed for their rights, including their sexual rights.

Thus the 1970s became a decade of greater openness about sexuality and growing acceptance of the rights of those who were not necessarily young adult heterosexual, married, and able-bodied to enjoy their sexuality. This "right" was reinforced by the 1973 Supreme Court decision legalizing abortion and by a growing number of states rescinding laws against various forms of private, consensual sexual activity among adults. In essence, the trend was to free sex of its reproductive imperative. Society's reproductive bias, which considers the only normal, healthy, natural, moral and legal sexual activities to be those which could conceivably lead to a socially approved pregnancy, was breaking down. The movement in this direction was described by a number of prominent sex researchers, at the invitation of Lester A. Kirkendall, in "New Bill of Sexual Rights an Responsibilities" (1976). Their proposal called for the abolition of the reproductive bias and supported the rights of all people to sexual expression as long as they do not harm others or interfere with their rights. This, and other movements of the '70s, demanded that Americans have rights to sexual expression along the same lines as those we take for granted for speech, religion and the press.

As might have been expected, however, these changes did not occur without opposition. From Anita Bryant, Phyllis Schlafly to Jerry Falwell, there have been campaigns to block those movements which violate the reproductive bias. Social change is often cyclical. As we proceed into the 1980s, one can sense a change in society's sexual temper. Indeed, 1980 elections may signal a return to a previous ethos. The moral majority's call for a national commitment to "family values" and a "right to life" is in essence a demand for a reinstatement of the reproductive bias. Sex as seen by this vocal political force is the exclusive perogative of adult married couples and is inextricably bound to reproduction and "Christian" values. There is reason to believe that there is considerable popular—and political—support for this return to the "old values." How does social work relate to these changes?

Social Work and Sexual Values

Because of the nature of the people it serves, social workers have inevitably come into contact with sex-related problems. And, as practitioners of a value-oriented field, have inevitably explored the nature of human sexuality and the meaning of its expression in everyday life. Yet relatively little was written about sexuality in social work texts or journals until the revolution of the early seventies.

Just about the same time as the Stonewall riot and the publication of *Human Sexual Inadequacy*, articles discussing the general nature of social work practice and education involvement with sex-related problems began to appear. Initially the literature was simply a plea for social workers to match society's growing openness about sexuality, assume a more assertive stance in dealing with these issues on a case-by-case basis and, perhaps, to begin to deal with broader sex-related social issues. (Gochros, 1971).

As the decade progressed, a modified orientation to sexual problems began to take form. Social workers began to perceive themselves as having a special commitment to the sexually oppressed. In the last few years, our approaches to these groups have become more fully developed and sophisticated. We have gone beyond the flag-waving of sexual liberation, to a more solid, if less dramatic exploration of how we can be of help to the groups we serve.

One of the most sexually oppressed of these groups, and one of the largest, is composed of children and adolescents. These individuals encounter oppression on two fronts: first, their sexual needs are often overlooked or suppressed and second, because of their vulnerability they are easy and frequent targets of sexual exploitation and abuse.

It is appropriate that this first issue of the *Journal of Social Work & Human Sexuality,* itself a symbol of social work's commitment to deal with sex-related problems, should focus on the sex-related problems of this ubiquitous sexually oppressed group.

What, then are some of the sex-related problems of children and adolescents and how might social workers address them?

Sexual Problems of Children and Adolescents

It is ironic that one of the largest, and certainly most beloved of our society's minority groups, our children and adolescents, profited little from the liberalization of sexual attitudes. Many, if not most adults still believe that children and adolescents are, or should be, asexual. Adults have difficulty accepting the youths around them as people having legitimate sexual feelings and who very likely engage in sexual activities. Our culture's prevailing attitude is that sex is a right and a legitimate need only for responsible adults. Children should stick to their games.

Sexual pleasure has not been seen as a legitimate right nor an appropriate joy of youth in American society. There are a number of reasons for this limitation. Being sexually active does not quite conform to our Rousseauian concept of the trouble-free virtuous youth. Children, it is believed, must be protected from the filth commonly associated in our society with sex. It soils the image of freshness and beauty which is considered part of childhood. But more significantly, it violates the demands of the reproductive bias, which limits sex to people who are in a position to bring about socially approved pregnancies. Overt sexual activity among children is frequently perceived as pathological. Masturbation and homosexual activities, both common activities among children, are still condemned by many as either sinful, sick or, at best, undesirable, and heterosexual experimentation is thought of as potentially catastrophic. Most adults tend to ignore childhood sexual needs, at least prior to the late teens, in the hopes that the behavior will simply go away. Thus, children have essentially been denied any sexual rights or privileges by virtually all classifications of adults, parents, ministers, teachers, and professional helpers.

The sexual rights of youth are beginning to be explored, however. Freud, himself, was an early champion, and to some extent, victim of the exploration of childhood sexuality. When he argued in Vienna at the turn of the century that "even" children were very much sexual human beings, he was rebuked by his medical colleagues. By then childhood had been so institutionalized that even those in the helping professions could not accept such adult behavior in innocent children. By contrast, sexual expression among children has been condoned and accepted in other cultures and other centuries. In some cultures, for example, infants are tranquilized by their parents stimulating their sex organs, very much as Americans insert bottles or pacifiers in their babies' mouths. Some cultures take account of the fact that adolescents into their early teens tend not to be too fecund and thus are tolerant of adolescent heterosexual activities. (However, as we all know not *all* young adolescents are totally sterile).

The issue of just what are the sexual rights and needs of the young will no doubt be debated for years to come. However, many of the sexual problems of childhood and adolescence continue to come from our society's difficulty in accepting their sexuality, and providing safe, responsible nonexploitative means for its expression.

Sexual Tasks of Childhood Adolescence

There is considerable overlay of the sex-related problems of adolescence and childhood. The division between childhood and adolescence is arbitrary, culturally determined and largely theoretical. The transition from adolescence to adulthood is even more ephemeral. If the major criterion for adulthood is achieving financial independence, then many college educated people maintain some semblance of adolescence well into their twenties. Indeed with the progressively earlier onset of puberty, and the extended period of financial dependence, adolescence is subsuming a progressively larger segment of people, at least in the contemporary American middle class.

A basic problem of that sizeable segment of our society is that those who have power over them (teachers, lawmakers, ministers, parents, professional helpers) tend to perceive them as being not old enough to have the right to sexual enjoyment, the ability to make sexual decisions, or the power to prevent their own sexual exploitation.

Until recently, adolescents' greater freedom and opportunities, growing capacity for procreation, relative vulnerability to adults, along with the reproductive bias led to the assumption that there were three tasks for those charged with the care and control of the young related to their sexuality:

1. to minimize the probability of their engaging in sexual activities, especially coitus;
2. to inculcate in them appropriate sex role behavior and an acceptance of the reproductive bias;
3. to protect them from sexual encounters with exploitative adults.

The rationales for these three tasks were fairly clear:

1. Sexual activities could lead to damaging results, ranging from the tragedy of an unwanted pregnancy to contracting sexually transmitted diseases. Further, youth could not make responsible decisions and might come to regret their choices. A major rationale for taking on this task was the conviction that well adjusted youth were not yet legitimate sexual human beings. Interest in sex was seen as problematic. Recently some authorities have accepted the sexuality of youth; the older the youth the more acceptable their sexuality. But the acceptance of sexual activities has been cautious and highly conditional (e.g., masturbation is all right. . .if not excessive; homosexual activities may be overlooked if transitory, sex play is all right if it doesn't go too far).
2. Children and adolescents must be acculturated into prevailing social sexual norms and be prepared for the assumption of appropriate adult sexual roles. Essentially this has included a denial of sexual activities while preparing the youth, especially males, to become sexually active and competent in heterosexual intercourse in the context of marriage. Youth are guided away from inappropriate sex role behaviors (what is desirable

sensitivity for a girl is undesirable sissy behavior for a boy. What is inappropriate aggressiveness for a boy is being too pushy for a girl). They are channeled to play and socialize in same sex relationships, but not allowed too much intimacy. The message is somewhat muddy: be heterosexually competent, but not now.

3. The third task of adults is to protect the child from the exploitation of adults who might try to meet their own sexual needs by taking advantage of relatively naive and powerless youth.

As the reproductive bias begins to fade, do these perceptions of the needs of children and adolescents still hold up? And do they adequately describe the range of problems of the youth in contemporary America?

It is impossible for children and adolescents not to be affected by the changing sexual world around them. Perhaps the most palpable change in the area of sexuality in the last generation has been its growing openness. Sex was never really invisible to youth, but certainly it is far less hidden today than it was only 20 or 30 years ago. One need only sample movies, television programs and popular music, and compare them with those of the 1950s to see some vivid changes. In today's media, pre-marital sex, abortion, recreational sex without ongoing relationships, and homosexuality are presented as viable options. This does not represent a weakness of censorship or a decrease in morality as much as it does the acceptance of sexual diversity among large segments of our society. Youth cannot escape an awareness of this value.

It is, however, this openness about differences in sexual options which creates some of the basic problems of today's youth. Parents, clergy, and other professional helpers are no longer, if they ever were, the primary producers or communicators of adult sexual values for youth. Children and adolescents are exposed to a range of opinions on all sides.

Thus, some longstanding perceptions of the sexuality of youth are being re-evaluated. Let's re-examine the three traditional responsibilities of adults regarding the sexuality of youth which were described above.

1. Minimizing the probability of youth engaging in sexual activities. If adolescents have sexual feelings (and they do) what is

their right to express them? What channels are appropriate and satisfying? There is little evidence to suggest that voluntary childhood sexual experiences necessarily impair adult sexual satisfaction. Furthermore, childhood and adolescent sexual experience is so ubiquitous that it seems foolhardy, if not pointless, to attempt to suppress it. Might not our role as helping professionals be to permit, or even encourage the right of youth to enjoy their sexuality in nonharmful and nonexploitive contexts? In situations in which institutional staff have a direct bearing on the sexual expressions of youth, this issue becomes even more inescapable. I was asked a few years ago by a visiting social worker in charge of a large correctional facility for adolescents in Sweden, "How do you American social workers provide for the sexual needs of the children in your institutions?" I had no answer.

2. To inculcate in youth an appreciation of the reproductive bias and promote appropriate sex role behaviors. This task becomes increasingly difficult and much more questionable as the support for the reproductive bias lessons. Sexual expression no longer needs to be limited to situations leading to socially approved pregnancies, and our youth need not be trained to be the standard bearers for this bias in the future. Although values of appropriate, responsible, joyful, caring sexual expression must be communicated; a sex-positive value system must replace a sex-negative one. And certainly our old standards of rigid sex role dimorphism are being called into question. Our definitions of "what is a man" and "what is a woman" are undergoing considerable changes. Out task would seem to be to help youth carefully develop, enunciate and glory in their uniqueness.

3. Protect youth from sexual encounters with exploitative adults. This is a difficult subject which excites considerable emotion on the part of adults. The chapters which follow will explore the complex issues and problems associated with the sexual abuse of children and adolescents. Few things arouse our anger and protective instincts as much as the thought of a adult "taking advantage" of a relatively powerless child or adolescent. Sexual molestation, abuse and exploitation are among the most pressing concerns of those involved with child welfare. This concern usually involves two aspects—how to prevent, or at least avoid repetition of such offenses by inter-

ventions with the adult. And secondly, how to help the child and adolescent who has been sexually exploited. However, there is a third issue: to what extent does the very depth of our concern itself create problems? For example, in the case of exhibitionists and even sexual molesters, the over-reaction of adults may create as much anxiety and trauma as the sexual experience itself. A calm, low-key, empathic evaluation of a child's reaction to a sexual experience may be the best guide to interventions with the child.

But beyond our concern to protect children and adolescents and help them conform to social expectations, there is yet another role in which social workers can make a significant contribution to the developing sexual human beings in their charge.

Enhancing Sexual Functioning in Youth

There is little written about the sexually well-functioning child and adolescent. Much, of course, has been written about *preparing* children and adolescents to be sexually functional adults, but exactly what youths are supposed to be doing while waiting to be adults is not quite clear.

Our concepts of sexual functioning are usually related to the context of heterosexual intercourse. There are many negative sanctions against youth adolescents engaging in intercourse, yet we offer them little in the way of alternatives or realistic guidelines. Actually, most of the ideas of what is, and more likely, what is *not* acceptable behavior reflect what is comfortable and even convenient for adults who care for them.

Specifying desirable sexual behavior for youth is quite difficult. Further, children of varying ages and emotional capacities seem to have various degrees of freedom and capacity for sexual activities. Without going into a detailed chronology of sexual needs and rights (which obviously vary depending on such factors as time, place, culture and individual growth patterns), I can only suggest some guidelines to consider in order to enhance the sexual functioning of children and adolescents.

1. *Privacy*—In most segments of our society, privacy is increasingly regarded as a basic human right. Sexual expression in our culture is considered private. Parents and caretakers can

and should support the child's right to privacy. Institutions tend to be crowded. Nevertheless, from time to time adolescents in institutions have a need to be alone, without the risk of unexpected intrusions. As they grow older, adolescents have an increasing right to the privacy of their sexual lives. It becomes their choice what to share of their thoughts and experiences with adults.

2. *Masturbation*—Masturbation can be a useful, pleasant activity for people of all ages. When we take into account the limited sexual options open to most children and adolescents, masturbation can be seen as especially valuable. Our society is moving beyond a concern about its harmful effects to the point of almost encouraging it for not only children and adolescents but adults as well. It relieves tension, provides a vehicle for enriching fantasies and an opportunity to learn more about one's own sexual resources and capacities.

3. *Homosexual Activity*—Homosexual activities are common among children in all cultures. Relatively few children who participate in these experiences end up exlusively homosexually oriented. Repeated studies show that no single factor including childhood sexual experiences *causes* a person be come homosexually oriented. Many children and adolescents participate in same-sex experiences out of curiosity, or for the sake of adventure. In institutions, the closeness of many same aged, same-sex individuals and the dilution of other intimate relationships increase the probability of homosexual activity occurring. A study by Halleck and Hersko (1962), for example, found that 69 percent of the adolescent girls in a training school were involved in some kind of homosexual behavior. Many, of course, find same-sex activities pleasurable and fulfilling. Some adolescents will repeat these experiences and become homosexually or ambisexually oriented adults. However, few experts in the mental health field consider such an orientation "pathological" or even problematic unless those in their environment (including social workers) make it so. Efforts to prevent same-sex activities in private may create more problems by intimidating children, by preventing them from being close to people of the same sex, and by introducing homophobic ideas. Rather, we must begin to explore how we might help homosexually oriented adolescents accomplish the

unique developmental tasks which they must accomplish in order to achieve a satisfying life.

4. *Heterosexual Activity*—Whether it's playing doctor, spin the bottle or post office, heterosexual experimentation is common and for obvious reasons. Play generally helps to prepare children and adolescents for adult roles. But it can also be pleasurable, exciting and fulfilling in the here and now. It can provide a sense of adequacy, an orientation to the joyful aspects of sex and an opportunity to try out skills in relating to the same and other sex. Almost all people "survive" sexual activities in adolescence, unless they are coerced into those activities.

Achieving these goals for the children and adolescents for whom social workers are providing services calls for a full range of traditional social work roles, from advocate to policy maker, and from clinician to educator. We can only suggest here some of the activities social workers might undertake in order to be more effective in overcoming the sexual oppression of children.

How Social Workers Can Help

1. Sexual exploitation and abuse of children is a primary target. The articles which follow comprehensively explore the social work tasks called for when a case of sexual abuse is discovered. At this point I will only emphasize what everyone who works in sexual abuse knows: The child who is abused is part of a much broader system which often both contributes to and sustains the abuse. This sytem not only includes the abused child and the abusing adult, but may involve the rest of the family, family friends and reference groups and perhaps the broader society in which these individuals live. Intervention must be directed toward the total system if it is going to be effective in terminating the abuse of the child, reintegrating the child into a nurturing environment and preventing possible subsequent abuse of siblings or others.
2. Social workers must be involved in developing useful realistic and humane sex education programs for children. Such programs must take into account the facts that children are vulnerable, impressionable, and uninformed, and vary in their

sexual orientations, needs and experiences. They often don't know what they don't know and therefore, we cannot wait until they ask the right questions. Unless contraindicated, the best sources of sex education usually are parents and regular adult caretakers. Often, however, these adults need and will accept support and guidance from social workers. When called upon to give this guidance, the social worker might consider that effective sex education goes well beyond reproductive education, and should not be perceived as simply an insurance policy against moral disaster. Rather it might best be designed to help children develop positive attitudes about their bodies and their sexuality with consideration of responsible ways in which their sexuality can be expressed. Sexuality in this sense involved not only physical pleasure but expressions of intimacy and identity. Generally parents can help children make responsible sexual choices by sharing their perceptions of what society expects of youth, their own candid opinions about sexual behavior and finally, their acceptance of the fact that as children grow older they will increasingly be making their own sexual choices. It is probably not too farfetched for parents or social workers to build some assertive training into the sex education they provide for children. All too often children are raised by parents and teachers to be acquiescent if not submissive to adults. A "good" child is one who follows instructions and does what she or he is told to do. There are ominous implications of this orientation when related to sex. Children and adolescents should be taught when and how to say "no" to adults and others when they sense they are being exploited.

3. While we generally think of children living in the midst of a nuclear family, it should be remembered that thousands of children and adolescents live in congregate care programs and institutions. Life in these settings compounds the already complex sex-related problems encountered by most adolescents (Shore and Gochros, 1981). Social workers are frequently involved with these programs and could offer significant help by considering the specific sexual issues and problems likely to be encountered by such institutional populations as the retarded, emotionally disturbed, physically handicapped, chronically ill and adjudicated delinquent, and assertively offering individual and group services to deal with these problems.

Finally, social workers must be clear about their own sexual values if they are going to be effective in helping children and parents cope with the complex issues related to childhood sexuality. Confusion and ambivalence about sexual matters often leads social workers to retreat from sex-related problems and to pretend that the problems don't exist. While there are variations in certain sexual values from region to region, religion to religion and over time, certain values implicit in social work ethics and values remain clear. These must provide the base and direction for social work practice to overcome the sexual oppression of children.

REFERENCES

Gochros, H. Sexual Problems in Social Work Practice, *Social Work,* 16(1), 1971.
Gochros, H. The Sexually Oppressed, *Social Work, 17,* (2), 1972.
Gochros, H. & Gochros J. *The Sexually Oppressed.* New York: Association Press, 1977.
Halleck, S. L. & Hersko, M. Homosexual Behavior in a Correctional Institution for Adolescent Girls, *American Journal of Orthopsychiatry,* 32, (5), 1962, 911–17.
Kinsey, A., Martin, C., & Pomeroy, W. *Sexual Behavior in the Human Male.* New York: W. B. Saunders, 1948.
Kirkendall, L. A. New Bill of Sexual Rights and Responsibilities, *The Humanist,* Jan./Feb., 1976.
Masters, W. Repairing the Conjugal Bed, *Time,* May 25, 1970.
Masters, W. & Johnson, V. *Human Sexuality Inadequacy.* Boston: Little Brown, 1970.
Shore, D., & Gochros, H. *Sexual Problems of Adolescents in Institutions.* Springfield, Ill.: Charles C. Thomas, 1981.

KNOWNS AND UNKNOWNS
IN SEXUAL ABUSE OF CHILDREN

Susan Meyers Chandler, DSW

The knowledge base in many areas of social work practice is still fragmented, sometimes unreliable, and often contains contradictory "findings." The literature on the sexual abuse of children is still a potpourri of untested theories, poorly designed studies, single-case insights, and a research tradition based on small clinical samples, making generalizations difficult and resulting in a weak knowledge base for social work practice. This paper will attempt to help social work practitioners consider the major findings of the current research on the sexual abuse of children.

Barriers to Knowledge About Sexual Abuse of Children

There are several factors which impede the progress of research on sexually assaulted children. The understandable concern of professionals about confidentiality often makes data collection on child victims difficult. Victims are often unable or unwilling to report their own victimization; thus there is an unknown proportion of sexually abused children who never become subjects in a research design. Public stigma which surrounds sexual misdeeds often creates a "conspiracy of silence" among family members, friends, and even some professionals who thus never report or discuss a known sexual abuse incident.

A more general challenge which inhibits scientific development in this field is the contrast between clinical reporting of case material which is then generalized to form typologies of sexual abuse (e.g., Burgess and Holmstrom, 1974, 1979; Schultz, 1975, 1980) and empirical research which uses a large sample of victims and statistical research methods to analyze the components of a particular problem. When clinicians and researchers are attempting to understand a complex phenomenon, like the impact of sexual abuse on children, they may often come to different conclusions, based on different data sets, different perspectives and knowledge-generating procedures.

And when social workers attempt to survey the literature, seeking knowledge from which to apply practice, these differences in approach may become confusing and the practitioner is left with studies which seem to contradict one another. This paper will offer some interpretations about why some of these differences occur and try to identify some of the consistent findings.

What is sex abuse? A review of the research on sexual abuse immediately confronts the problem of *what* is the range of activity to be defined.

Katz and Mazur's (1979) extensive review of the research on sexual abuse demonstrates that most of the studies on "rape" often include a variety of sexual activities ranging from completed forcible rape, exluding attempted rape (Amir, 1971; MacDonald, 1971; Schiff, 1969); completed rapes including attempted rape (Chappell, Geis, and Geis, 1977; Hursch and Selkin, 1974); forcible rape, attempted rape, oral and anal sex (Burgess and Holmstrom, 1974; DeFrancis, 1969; Peters, 1973, 1976); sodomy, impairing morals (DeFrancis, 1969); statutory rape (Goldberg and Goldberg, 1976; Hayman, Lanza Fuentes, and Algor, 1972); to fondling and caressing children (Peters, 1973, 1976). Under "sexual assualt studies," there is even a broader range of activities and types of offenses described. These studies may include noncoercive sexual relations between a child and an adult (Bender and Blau, 1937); fondling, indecent exposure, including exhibition (Burtin, 1968); homosexual experiences (Gagnon, 1965); and exhibition, genital petting, and manipulation by adults on children (Kinsey, Pomeroy, Martin, and Bebhard, 1953). With these vastly differing definitions of the "problem," it is extremely difficult to find reported similarities regarding typologies of victims, or agreement as to the emotional impact of the abuse on the child. A major problem here is the uncritical use of statutory categories of behavior which are intended for legal and not clinical purposes. Clearly, the first task in understanding sexual abuse of a child is to delineate the types of sexual activities children experience and examine the forms separately. This, however, is rarely done.

Related to this problem of defining what is sexual abuse is a belief that sexual abuse is not harmful. Many have argued that the effect of victimization upon children has been exaggerated in the earlier literature (Gagnon, 1965; Schultz, 1975) and that up to 60 percent of the children fully participated, collaborated, or "seduced" the adult partner (Gebhard, Gagnon, Pomeroy, and Christenson, 1965; Bender and Grugett, 1952; Weiss, Rogers, Darwin, and Dutton, 1955). Schultz contends that many victimized children are seeking out or allowing affectionate behavior from their adult partners and that many feel kindly and lovingly towards them (Schultz, 1975). While this may be a clinician's experience with several children, survey research, which systematically assesses patterns of behavior from a large number of sexually victimized persons, suggests a vastly different experience for children. Finkelhor (1979) found in his sample of 796 persons that coercion (including force) was present in over half (58 percent) of the sexual experiences of children and that only a tiny fraction of the respondents said that they had initiated or voluntarily participated in the sexual activity with an older partner. Over half of the female resondents reported being frightened by the experience. Several respondents acknowledged that the physical sensations "felt good," and remembered a "closeness" not frequently experienced. Yet they often put these feelings in the context of "an overwhelming sense of helplessness, guilt, anger, or fear" (Finkelhor, 1979, p. 66). Sixty-six percent of the women in Finkelhor's study rated the experience as negative, while only 7 percent rated it as positive. On a five-point scale from 1 (positive) to 5 (negative), the mean for all females was 4.0. Boys reported feeling less traumatized by the sexual contact. Thirty-eight percent of the male respondents rated their overall experience as negative. The other male respondents expressed some interest and seemed to be less frightened or shocked by the sexual acts.

Clinical versus research knowledge. It is important to underscore that there are different knowledge-generating approaches to understand a problem. Clinical observation provides rich and detailed case material from which a practitioner can learn and develop theories about the types of persons who are typically seen as victims, the dynamics of particular cases, the types of activities which can be most traumatizing, and the types of therapies or counseling strategies which seem to successfully reduce stress and bring about healthy functioning. Clinical observations, which are usually based on small samples, are extremely important in a clinician's own practice and in generating questions to be investigated through research. However, they have a potential for a variety of weaknesses such as reporting biased and selective findings based on small samples. The researcher, on the other hand, searches systematically for observable trends among a large sample of victims, seeking to uncover patterns or similarities generalizable to a wider population. These endeavors may be influenced by a number of methodological difficulties.

Empirical research findings continue to be inconsistent and limited because the variables studied and the definitions of the problem often differ from study to study.

Another methodological problem is the issue of underreporting. While most writers estimate that perhaps only 10 percent of victims ever report their assault to an authority, such as the police or a social agency, most of the research data come from reported cases. Thus we are learning about a small and perhaps atypical group of victimized persons. Most studies, with large sample sizes from which generalizations are possible, are drawn from hospitals and emergency rooms. These cases are usually reported shortly after the assault and are often associated with physical injuries. This may not be the typical pattern for children and adolescents who, if they report to anyone, may report their assault to a teacher or a friend. In many cases, the victimization is inadvertently "discovered" through other social work intervention processes. These cases are rarely documented or studied. Thus, information about these cases is largely unknown.

Retrospective studies of subjects from the general population also have methodological problems. Finkelhor's (1979) study of the general population reported shockingly large numbers of both childhood and adolescent coerced sexuality (i.e., one in eleven boys and one in five girls). This research attempts to estimate actual frequencies of sexual abuse in a cross section of a population (thus including cases never before reported) as opposed to collecting data on existing and known cases. However, this type of research may report inflated numbers since subjects are asked to remember sexual incidents and some could redefine an earlier voluntary but unpleasant sexual encounter as having coercive elements.

The small numbers of victims studied in most of the published research limits the data analyses possible. Multivariate statistical techniques, which can isolate important indicators within complex phenomena, require relatively large numbers of respondents. For example, multivariate analyses conducted with sample of 400 adults and children indicate that the previous mental health status of the victim is the single most important predictor of acute emotional trauma associated with sexual abuse (Ruch and Chandler, 1981). This finding remains even when several assault variables, such as the extent of injuries sustained, the number of assailants encountered, and the previous relationship with the offender (excluding father-daughter incest), are controlled for. This research also indicates that victims who had been victimized previously are significantly *less* traumatized than first-time victims even when previous mental health status is controlled for. Thus, victims seem to develop coping skills subsequent to an assault that helps them withstand a second sexual abuse. Only with large samples can variables such as these be analyzed and models of trauma designed. Additionally, few studies employ control procedures (e.g., control of comparison groups and control variables) which make it possible to draw meaningful conclusions.

What Is the Incidence of Sexual Abuse of Children?

While all persons are at risk of some form of sexual abuse, adolescents and young adults are at highest risk of coerced sexual intercourse. Children are most vulnerable to all other forms of sexual abuse. Children typically keep their sexual victimization a secret from their parents or significant others (Landis, 1956; Peters, 1976), and even when children do inform their parents, the parents often are reluctant to inform the authorities. Thus, most knowledge about childhood sexual abuse is learned from adults recalling a sexual victimization which occurred in childhood. Aware of the difficulties in this type of recall, the frequence of childhood sexual assault reported in the research literature ranges from 19 percent of the adult females surveyed (Finkelhor, 1979) to 35 percent of a college sample who recalled being a victim of a sexual assault by an adult male (Landis, 1956).

Finkelhor's (1979) large study surveyed 796 college-aged students and examined their reports of clearly defined, sexual experiences encountered as children. While there is a limit to the generalizability of this sample, this study is more likely to uncover previously unreported cases and avoids the bias of clinical samples. This study demonstrates clearly what has been reported throughout the literature—that children are at high risk for sexual assault and that female children are at much greater risk than male children. In this sample, 19.2 percent of the women surveyed had been in a sexual encounter as a child with an adult partner. Half of these experiences were between a child twelve and under and an adult eighteen and over. Among the males surveyed, 8.6 percent of the sample had been in a sexual encounter with an older partner. The potential for a white, middle-class bias in this type of survey technique suggests that the numbers of child victims may be even greater if lower-class subjects were included. These people are known to be victimized more frequently by other forms of violent crimes, and it is likely that they do not escape sexual assault. DeFrancis (1969) notes that, while female children are believed to be at a much greater risk than male children, the number of male child victims may be disproportionately underreported due to even greater stigma attached to male child victimization.

Even the best designed and confidential survey research cannot delineate the "true" number of child victims when the respondents are unwilling to report such an event. Yet, even after noting all of the methodological problems in collecting this type of data and understanding the inherent biases of volunteer population, the existence of childhood sexual encounters with adult partners is surprisingly widespread. The research evidence demonstrates that sexual abuse of children is prevalent across society; that it most commonly occurs among children under twelve; it is perceived as negative by the majority of victims; and it is more common among children whose families are experiencing marital conflict and family disruption (Finkelhor, 1979). The majority of the abuse includes threats and force (Ruch, Chandler, and Harter, 1980); the offender is known to the child (DeFrancis, 1969); and almost half of the children report multiple episodes (Finkelhor, 1979). Data on social class, race, and ethnicity seem to be dependent on (and potentially biased by) sampling procedures. College student samples are skewed toward white middle-class subjects, whereas samples from child protective service agencies or emergency rooms at public hospitals have an overrepresentation of lower-class and ethnic and minority victims. Amir's finding (1971) in Philadelphia that 82.5 percent of the offenders and 80.5 percent of the victims were black clearly was a result of inappropriate sampling. Ruch and Chandler (1978), sampling from a public sex abuse treatment center, found over 68 percent of the victims to be Caucasian in a community which was only 30 percent Caucasian. The presumed underreporting of ethnic victims, as well as the known differential social service utilization of certain population groups, limits the ability to know about the demographic characteristics of sexaully abused child victims. With the preceding issues in mind, the remainder of this chapter will discuss the main research findings which have been replicated and thus may be cautiously used to help direct social work practice with sexually abused children.

Major Findings

Age and sexual abuse. Glaister (1973) found the most common age for the sexual abuse of children to be between the years of 7 and 12 Burton (1968) found the model category to be between 7 and 10. Burgess and Holmstrom (1974), using a maximum age of 16, found 37 percent of the victims were 12 years or under. Unfortunately, the data on the age of child victims depend to some extent on the age maximum used in the researchers' definition. Finkelhor's frequency data (1979) found the mean age for girls to be 10.2 and for boys, 11.2. These data do suggest that young children are vulnerable to victimization. These data also challenge those who contend that many victims are sexually mature, have developed secondary sexual characteristics, and may be "practicing" seductive behavior which encourages the adult partner (Gagnon, 1965).

The data indicate that the risk of sexual abuse *decreases* for young women before puberty, and this may correspond not with their sexual awakening but rather with their ability to act assertively and be more able to successfully resist unwanted sexual activity. However, Ruch and Chandler (1978) found an increasing rate of children over thirteen reporting non-familial rape. This trend may reflect an increased concern among older girls regarding the possibility of pregnancy and venereal disease. Older victims assaulted by a non-family member presumably have a greater cognizance of the meaning of forced sexuality and their own vulnerability. Another point of concern is that victims of incest often do not report for months and sometimes years after the initial victimization has occurred; thus the age of the victim at the time of the report may be substantially higher than the age at which the victimization actually occurred. This may partially explain the discrepancies among the research findings on the age of the sexually victimized child.

Relationship to the offender. One finding that is reported consistently in the literature on the sexual abuse of children is that most offenders are known to their victims (Elwell, 1979). In the majority of cases, the offenders are family members, friends, or neighbors. In 76 percent of the cases reported by the Finkelhor (1979) respondents, the child knew the offender, and in 43 percent of the cases, the offender was a family member. A similar pattern was found among the boys. Seventy percent of the male victims knew their partners prior to the assault, and 17 percent were family members. DeFrancis (1969) reported 77 percent of the children knew their partner; Goldberg and Goldberg (1976) reported 74 percent of their sample knew their partner. The studies which include adult women in their samples tend to have a larger percent of stranger rapists. Hayman et al. (1972) reported that 60 percent of the victims which included children and women were raped by a stranger. The data is strikingly clear that the percentage of victims sexually abused by a stranger largely depends on the age group of the victims studied and increases as the age of the victims increases.

Emotional trauma associated with sexual abuse. The traumatizing effects of rape and other forms of sexual abuse have been clearly established in a variety of recent studies utilizing diverse methodologies (Burgess and Holmstrom, 1974, 1979; Fox and Scherl, 1972). Burgess and Holmstrom (1974, 1979) found that sexual assault victims experience a trauma syndrome which consists of an acute phase immediately following the assault where the victim's primary reponse is fear and confusion and a longer-term reorganization phase characterized by anxiety, fear, somatic changes, interpersonal difficulties, and major changes in life-style (Holmstrom and Burgess, 1978).

The victim's concerns may be focused on physiological aspects such as the medical injury, venereal disease, pregnancy, or social-psychological problems such as interpersonal and familial relationships. Most research studies have conceptualized the emotional trauma associated with sexual abuse in terms of the symptoms exhibited (e.g., depression, anxiety, fear). Ruch et al. (1980) conceptualize sexual assault trauma as having two theoretically distinct dimensions. First, the *type* of trauma which refers to the nature of the concern or problem the victim is experiencing (e.g., anger, depression) and, second, the *level* of trauma which documents the degree to which the person is affected by victimization (e.g., mild reaction to extremely severe reaction). Very little data have been collected with this specificity; thus emotional trauma is often used as an important, clinical relevant dependent variable, but it is rarely clearly defined.

Finkelhor (1979) developed a scale to measure the degree (level) of emotional trauma for each respondent who reported an incident of sexual abuse. The scale rated the sexual experience from positive to negative. He concludes that the larger the age differences between the child and the adult offender the more severe the level of trauma. If the adult was more than ten years older than the child, the experience was quite negative. However, when several variables were entered into a regression equation to discover which single variable is the best predictor of emotional trauma, instances in which physical force was used explains most of the child's negative reactions to the sexual contact. The respondents who recalled the experiences as most traumatizing usually recalled coercion and aggression. If this is correct, then earlier theories which argue that emotional scarring and trauma are primarily caused by the child's sense of guilt (McFarlane, 1978), presumed participation, or the reactions of an alarmed society (Schultz, 1975) are called into question.

Ruch and Chandler (1981) have also found that the presence of threats and force are important factors in understanding the dynamics of emotional trauma in childhood sexual assault. An important caveat, however, in applying these findings to intrafamilial sexual assaults is noted by almost all researchers. The assault experiences with close family members are consistently found to be more traumatic than those with acquaintances or strangers. It has been assumed that the closer the relationship the greater the violation of the child's trust and security, the more involved and complicated the family dynamics, and the more serious the taboo violated. Empirical research on reported cases as well as unreported cases supports the clinical data that father-daughter incest is the most traumatizing kind of childhood sexual abuse. Thus, while in non-family-related sexual abuse the age of the partner, the amount of force and coercion are important characteristics associated with emotional trauma, in most intrafamilial incidences there is very little physical force, yet the levels of trauma among incest cases are extremely high.

Common sense might hypothesize that victims who have been repeatedly assaulted over a long period of time would have heightened levels of traumas. Research evidence does not support this idea. Perhaps the first sexual victimization is the most traumatizing, and the more assertive children take actions to halt it. Others perhaps learn to endure the situation, and it becomes a part of an unhappy, dysfunctional, victimizing childhood. Ruch and Chandler (1981) found that a prior rape victimization is a significant predictor of lower levels of emotional trauma after a subsequent sexual assault and suggest that victims develop coping skills which may mitigate trauma.

Research focusing on incestuous relationships often examines the influence of the child's family background on the occurrence and degree of emotional trauma. Halleck (1965) noted that most victims come from families in which there was significant emotional distress and deprivation at the time of the attack. Spencer (1978) asserts that the primary cause of father-daughter incest is an emotionally unstable father. She contends that most perpetrators have paranoid personalities, are often alcoholics, and are insecure about their masculinity. But many articles on incest often include theories which "blame the mother" (Justice and Justice, 1979) either for relinquishing the mother role (Spencer, 1978), for being absent both physically and psychologically (Browning and Boatman, 1977), for exchanging roles with her daughter (Peters, 1976), or maintaining that the mother was a silent partner who is aware of the incest but does nothing to stop it (Forward and Buch, 1978). Many affirm that the mother must be the focus on the treatment of incestuous families. The declarations that the mother "colludes" or is "always aware of the incestuous activity" are myths nicely dispelled by Berliner (1977). She reminds us that the main task of the social worker is to protect the child from further abuse, which entails not only preventing the offender from continued access to the child, but also believing the child and not blaming the victim (or the mother) for the victimization.

Finkelhor's research (1979) puts these theories into focus based on empirical evidence. His data show that family disruption and conflict are associated with higher rates of sexual victimization among children. Children whose fathers were not living in the home are at higher risk for childhood victimization. Girls living without their mothers are at the greatest risk of nonfamilial sexual victimization. It is interesting to note that the increased vulnerability for children with absent mothers in the home is victimization with an older person, *not* incest. Disruptive, dysfunctional families do put children at risk, not only for mental health problems, but for childhood sexual abuse as well.

Reactions to sexual abuse. It is often surprising to learn that sexual intercourse, a goal in most adult sexual expression, occurred in only 4 percent of the childhood sexual victimizations reported by Finkelhor (1979) and in 25 percent of the cases reported by Conte and Berliner (1981). Forced masturbation and fondling of the genitals is more often the form of sexual activity which occurs between children and adult partners. Even when the sexual activity continues over a long time period, rarely does the adult partner attempt sexual intercourse. Mohr et al. (1964) contend that, while the opportunity for sexual intercourse is available to adults who sexually molest children, their interest in the child may represent an attempt to escape or avoid adult forms of sexuality and its "responsibilities." From the perspective of the child, the "lesser" forms of sexual activity, such as forced masturbation, digital penetration, oral-genital stimulation, seem to be equally as traumatizing and disturbing as sexual intercourse. There is an awareness that what is happening is not right (DeFrancis, 1969) and, regardless of the specific form of sexual activity, the child seems to feel fear, confusion, and an inability to protect herself or himself.

Finkelhor (1979) found that 63 percent of the female respondents and 73 percent of the males never told anyone about the experience; Rush (1974) and Peters (1976) argue that fear, confusion, and ignorance about what to do prevent most child victims from reporting the episode to an authority. Rather than children seeking and accepting sexual attention from an adult partner to fill a void in their lives (Schultz, 1975), most childhood sexual experiences are exploitative (Brownmiller, 1975; Clark and Lewis, 1977), and social workers need to be concerned about protecting children from such abuse.

Clinical observational studies have indicated a number of symptoms that develop after a sexual assault. Commonly there are mood changes, often nightmares, phobias, school problems, changes in behavior ranging from withdrawal to hyperactivity, changes in interpersonal relationships, and physical stress (Burgess and Holmstrom, 1974; Burton, 1968; Sgroi, 1978). Peters (1976) observed that in the early stages withdrawal was the most common symptom among child rape victims. DeFrancis (1969) found that the majority of the children interviewed had some pre-existing anxiety symptoms that were exacerbated after the sexual event. Weber (1977) and Brody-aga (1975) found that many runaways are children trying to escape from an unwanted sexual situation at home. Often children run away from home due to the lack of support received from significant persons in the child's life after they report a sexual assault. Depression, low self-esteem, and lack of self-worth were found among the majority of child victims studied by DeFrancis (1969), yet generally child victims showed fewer symptoms than adult rape victims (Burgess and Holmstron, 1974; Ruch and Chandler, 1981; Peters, 1976).

Most of the long-term data on the impact of sexually assaulted children comes from psychiatric case material. The literature is divided between those who conclude that there are few lasting effects of childhood sexual victimization (Bender and Blau, 1937; Gagnon, 1956) and those who believe that sexual assault often leaves permanent psychological damage (McCauldron, 1967; Peters, 1976). Summit and Kryso (1978) found that 90 percent of a sample of mothers seeking help for child abuse had themselves been sexually abused as children. However, this form of research has many methodological problems which make generalizations regarding the impact of long-lasting psychological damage difficult to assess. Since so few of the victims ever report their experiences, "data" on childhood sexual assault is biased in that only the reported cases are being examined. Then, when psychiatric caseloads are used to examine long-term emotional reactions, the data base becomes persons who are emotionally disturbed and also have been sexually assaulted. If childhood sexual abuse is as common as most of the data indicate, it is difficult to associate long-term emotional trauma with an incident of childhood sexual abuse without examining other factors.

Burgess and Holmstrom (1978) and Ruch and Chandler (1981) have reported the the preassault mental health status of a child influences his or her postassault adjustment more than any other single factor. That is, children who have already developed successful coping skills, are well adjusted in school, and have adequate interpersonal skills seem most able to cope with a sexual victimization. Prior mental health has been demonstrated to be an important factor in assessing the impact of rape in adult women as well (Ruch et al., 1980). While it may be almost tautological to state that the healthiest persons prior to sexual victimization become the healthiest victims, this does have several important implications for social work.

Ruch et al. (1980) clarified this association for adult women (in this case measured by life change events) and found that the relationship between prior life change and sexual assault trauma was curvilinear. That is, adult victims with no major life change events prior to an assault (and thus little opportunity to develop coping strategies) were highly traumatized by a sexual assault. Adult victims with a large number of life change events, which might indicate a dysfunctional life-style and emotional ill health and/or persons experiencing multiple external stresses, also were highly traumatized by a sexual assault. Victims with the lowest levels of assault trauma seem to be those who had experienced some stress in their lives and had learned from it or mastered it. The parallels with this finding may be applicable to child victims. If the degree of prior mental health functioning is an important factor for successful recovery from a sexual victimization, then social workers need to encourage health coping skills and work towards achieving high levels of mental health functioning among all children.

Sexual Assault as a Sexist Phenomenon

As social workers, we should look at childhood sexual abuse within a social context (Stevens, 1980; McIntyre, 1981; Butler, 1978). The fact of childhood sexual victimization is real. The fear of sexual assault affects all women. It inhibits their life-style, limits their freedom, and significantly influences the way they live their lives. The fear is well founded because no female is immune from sexual assault. Yet this pervasive social problem, which affects perhaps one in every five women, is often considered in the public mind as a "minor skirmish in the inevitable battle of the sexes" (Clark and Lewis, 1977). While women are often taught that rape is the worst thing that can happen to a person, many actors in the criminal justice system view rape as a natural consequence of the sexual game in which men pursue and women are pursued. And the charge of rape is often viewed with suspicion and an assumption that the female (or child) often lies. Research by LaFree (1980) and Chandler and Torney (1981) reported that the focus of most rape investigations is on the character of the *victim*, and there is clear evidence that the victim's characteristics such as previous sexual behavior, mental health status, and race determines the likelihood of the alleged *offender's* indictment and conviction. Few rape cases ever come to court, and most feminist-oriented rape centers are seriously questioning advising victims to testify in court since the victim most often is put on trial and the alleged offender most often is acquitted. Beginning with Griffin's (1971) assault on the prevailing attitudes towards rape and rape victims, data were being collected on females and how they, as victims, felt about the offense. Several articles carefully detailed the general thesis that rape is just another form of women's oppression in a sexist society which assumes the natural inequality of the sexes and the natural domination and superiority of the male (Clark and Lewis, 1977; McIntyre, 1981).

Victims of rape and incest often join in the "conspiracy of silence" which surrounds sexual abuse. It seems hard for this society to comprehend that huge numbers of women and children and a substantial number of male children are sexually assaulted. A prevailing notion is that rape is shameful and degrading act for its victims and the less they talk about it the better for all of us. Social workers who work with victims know that sexual assault is not an inevitable act which women and children must learn to live with. Social workers must begin to see that all forms of sexual abuse are *social,* not natural consequences of human nature. Social workers can take a lead in not only attempting to diminish the adverse consequences to the victims who report the abuse but also begin the investigation and analysis of the elements of society which "permit" sexual abuse to perpetuate. Brownmiller (1976) asserts that the basic reason for societal revenge associated with rape was the acceptance of the premise that sexual activity with a female to whom one had no legal access was not violating *her* rights but, rather, the rights of the man (husband or father) who owned her. Many early laws stated this clearly, in that the "humiliated male" was the one to receive restitution, not the violated female. The legacy of this type of assumption continues today. Many persons believe that women do not own their sexual and reproductive capacities. This logic leads to the situation in which men believe that women (and children) who say "no" really mean "yes" but are unable to express their genuine desire for sexuality out of "respect" for the dominant male in their life (i.e., their father or husband). This assumption also explains some of the beliefs that "seductive" and "provocative" women (and children) are persons wanting sexual contact but cannot admit it and often must lie about it.

Since the status of women (and children) as private, sexual, and reproductive property has created the problem of sexual abuse as we know it, it cannot be resolved until females are no longer accorded that status but are regarded as having the right to their sexual and reproductive autonomy. Social work must closely examine the institutional structures which perpetuate sexism in society and foster the ideology of inherent inequalities between the sexes. Social work, traditionally a women's profession, must actively work towards the transformation of women's legal and social status from inequality to equality within the social, legal, and economic structures of society. It is clear from the existence of prejudicial laws governing rape, abortion, and the absence of adequate equal pay legislation (not to mention the failure of the Equal Rights Amendment) that women have not yet fully emerged with equal status.

What Do We Need to Know?

This chapter has discussed how much we know and how well we know it. Despite what we know about childhood sexual abuse, there is still a great deal we do not know. A major research objective for the future is to acquire a national program of research on sexual abuse of children. Data must be systematically collected and analyzed so that the social characteristics of child victims and their offenders are obtained. Treatment typologies around specific social work intervention strategies need to be evaluated. Questions such as, "When is it advisable for the victim to become active in the prosecution of an offender?" need to be explored. Social workers need to know when the removal of the incest perpetrator (or the victim) from the family is in the best interest of the child. What information do we now have from clinical practice that can be assessed? For example, are groups of victims a more effective treatment strategy for children than individual therapies and counseling? For what types of incest victims is family therapy the most effective treatment strategy? What do we know about victims from ethnic and minority groups, and are the current treatments of choice adequately meeting the needs of these victims? How can we learn about the sexual victimization of children in middle and upper classes, who traditionally are underrepresented in the utilization of public mental health facilities and yet in survey samples represent a significant proportion of the victimized population? How can social workers better communicate with one another and other professionals working with abused children to share what is known and coordinate efforts to learn more? Many of these questions remain unanswered. Much is still unknown. Social work must begin to design and conduct research that will be both relevant to the clinical practitioner and to policy planners who develop programs and advocate for system and legal reform. We know a considerable amount about child sexual abuse and its effect on its victims, but we need to know much more. How do we successfully develop an accurate knowledge base to inform our practice? That is the challenge.

REFERENCES

Amir, M. *Patterns in Forcible Rape.* Chicago: University of Chicago Press, 1971.
Bender, L., and Blau, A. The Reaction of Children to Sexual Relations with Adults. *American Journal of Orthopsychiatry,* 1937, 7(4), 500–518.
Bender, L., and Grugett, A. E. A Follow-up Study of Children Who Had Atypical Sexual Experience. *American Journal of Orthopsychiatry,* 1952 22(4), 825–837.
Berliner, L. Child Sexual Abuse: What Happens Next. *Victimology,* 1977 2(2), 327–331.
Brodyaga, L. M. Rape and Its Victims: A Report for Citizens, Health Facilities and Criminal Justice Agencies. LEAA. U.S. Department of Justice. Washington, D.C.: U.S. Government Printing Office, 1975.
Browning, D., and Boatman, B. Incest: Children at Risk. *American Journal of Psychiatry,* 1977 34(1), 69–72.
Brownmiller, S. *Against Our Will: Men, Women and Rape.* New York: Simon and Schuster, 1975.
Burgess, A. W., and Holmstrom, L. L. *Rape: Crisis and Recovery.* Bowie, Maryland: Robert J. Bardy, 1979.
Burgess, A. W., and Holmstrom, L. L. *Rape: Victims and Crisis.* Bowie, Maryland: Robert J. Brady, 1974.
Burton, L. *Vulnerable Children.* London: Routledge and Kegal Paul, 1968.
Butler, S. *Conspiracy of Silence: The Trauma of Incest.* San Francisco: New Glide Publications, 1978.
Chandler, S., and Torney, M. Dyad and Decisions: The Processing of Rape Victims Through the Criminal Justice System. *The California Sociologist* (in press).
Chappell, D.; Geis, R.; and Geis, G. (eds.). *Forcible Rape: The Crime, the Victim and the Offender.* New York: Columbia University Press, 1977.
Clark, L., and Lewis, D. *Rape: The Price of Coercive Sexuality.* Toronto: The Women's Press, 1977.
Conte, J., and Berliner, L. Sexual Abuse of Children: Implications for Practice. *Social Casework,* 1981, 62 (10), 601–606.
DeFrancis, V. *Protecting the Child Victim of Sex Crimes Committed by Adults: Final Report.* Denver: The American Humane Association, 1969.
Elwell, M. E. Sexually Assaulted Children and Their Families. *Social Casework,* 1979 60(4), 227–235.
Finkelhor, D. *Sexually Victimized Children.* New York: The Free Press, 1979.

Fox, S.S. and Scherl, D.J. Crisis Intervention with Victims of Rape. *Social Work*, 1972, 17(1), 37–42.

Forward, S., and Buch, C. *Betrayal of Innocence: Incest and Its Devastation*. New York: Penguin Books, 1978.

Gagnon, J. H. Female Child Victims of Sex Offenses. *Social Problems*, 1965, 13(2), 176–192.

Gebhard, P. H.: Gagnon, J. H.; Pomeroy, W.; and Christenson, C. *Sex Offenders*. New York: Harper and Row, 1965.

Glaister, J. Medical Jurisprudence and Toxicology. E. Rentoul and H. Smith, eds. Baltimore: Williams and Wilkins, 1973, 425–459.

Goldberg, J. A., and Goldberg, R. W. *Girls on City Streets: A Study of 1400 Cases of Rape*. New York: Arna Press, 1976.

Griffin, S. Rape: The All-American Crime. *Ramparts*, 1971 (September), 26–35.

Halleck, S. L. Emotional Effects of Victimization. In R. Slovenho, ed., *Sexual Behavior and the Law*. Springfield, Ill.: Thomas, 1965, 673–686.

Hayman, C. R.; Lanza, C.; Fuentes, R.; and Algor, K. Rape in the District of Columbia. *American Journal of Obstetrics and Gynecology*, 1972, 113, 91–97.

Holstrom, L. L., and Burgess, A. W. *The Victim of Rape: Institutional Reactions*. New York: Wiley, 1978.

Hursch, C. J., and Selkin, J. Rape Prevention Research Project. Annual Report of the Violence Research Unit, Division of Psychiatric Service, Department of Health and Hospitals, Denver, Colorado, 1974.

Justice, B., and Justice, R. *The Broken Taboo: Sex in the Family*. New York: Human Sciences Press, 1979.

Katz, S., and Mazur, M. A. *Understanding the Rape Victim: A Synthesis of Research Findings*. New York: John Wiley & Sons, 1979.

Kinsey, A. C.; Pomeroy, W.; Martin, C.; and Gebhard, P. *Sexual Behavior in the Human Female*. Philadelphia: Saunders, 1953.

LaFree, G. The Effect of Sexual Stratification by Race on Official Reactions to Rape. *American Sociological Review*, 1980, 45(5), 842–854.

Landis, J. Experiences of 500 Children with Adult Sexual Deviation. *Psychiatric Quarterly Supplement*, 1956, 30, 91–109.

MacDonald, J. *Rape Offenders and Their Victims*. Springfield, Ill.: Charles C. Thomas, 1971.

McCauldron, R. J. Rape. *Canadian Journal of Corrections*, 1967, 9, 37–57.

McFarlane, K. Sexual Abuse of Children. In J.R. Chapman and M. Gates (eds.), *The Victimization of Women*. Beverly Hills, Calif.: Sage, 1978.

McIntyre. K. Role of Mothers in Father-Daughter Incest: A Feminist Analysis. *Social Work*, 1981, 26(6), 462–466.

Mohr, J. W.; Turner, R. E.; and Jerry, M. B. *Pedophilia and Exhibitionism: A Handbook*. Toronto: University of Toronto Press, 1964.

Peters, J. Children Who Are Victims of Sexual Assault and the Psychology of Offenders. *American Journal of Psychotherapy*, 1976, 30(3), 338–342.

Peters, J. Child Rape: Defusing a Psychological Time Bomb. *Hospital Physician*, February, 1973, 46–49.

Ruch, L. O., and Chandler, S. M. The Crisis Impact of Sexual Assault on Three Victim Groups: Adult Rape Victims, Child Rape Victims and Incest Victims. *Journal of Social Research*, 1981 (in press).

Ruch, L. O.; Chandler, S. M.; and Harter, R. Life Change and Rape Impact. *Journal of Health and Social Behavior*, 1980, 21(3), 248–259.

Ruch, L. O., and Chandler, S. M. The Sex Abuse Treatment Center Program Evaluation Report. Honolulu, Hawaii, February, 1978.

Rush, F. The Sexual Abuse of Children: A Feminist Point of View. In N. Connell and C. Wilson, eds. *Rape: The First Source Book for Women.* New York: New American Library, 1974, 65–75.

Schiff, A. Statistical Features of Rape. *Journal of Forensic Sciences,* 1977, 14, 102–111.

Schultz, L. G. Diagnosis and Treatment—Introduction in L. G. Scholtz (ed.). *The Sexual Victimology of Youth.* Springfield: Charles C. Thomas, 1980.

Schultz, L. G. The Child as a Sex Victim: Socio-Legal Perspectives. In L. G. Schultz (ed.). *Rape Victimology.* Springfield: Charles C. Thomas, 1975.

Sgroi, S. M. Child Sexual Assault: Some Guidelines for Intervention and Assessment. In A. W. Burgess, et al. (eds.). *Sexual Assault of Children and Adolescents.* Lexington, Mass.: Lexington, 1978, 129–142.

Spencer, J. Father-Daughter Incest: A Clinical View from the Corrections Field. *Child Welfare,* 1978, 57(9), 581–589.

Stevens, D. Dynamics of Victimization. A paper presented at the National Association of Social Workers First National Conference on Social Work Practice with Women. September, 1980.

Summit, R.; and Kryso, J. Sexual Abuse of Children: A Clinical Spectrum. *American Journal of Orthopsychiatry,* 1978 48(2), 237–251.

Weber, E. Sexual Abuse Begins at Home. *Ms.* April, 1977, 64–67.

Weiss, J. E.; Rogers, E.; Darwin, M.; and Dutton, C. A Study of Girl Sex Victims. *Psychiatric Quarterly,* 1955 29(1), 1–27.

TREATING CHILD SEXUAL ABUSE:
AN OVERVIEW OF CURRENT PROGRAM
MODELS

Kee MacFarlane, MSW
Josephine Bulkley, JD

The upsurge of interest in the problem of child sexual abuse over the past five years has resulted in the parallel growth of specialized treatment programs to deal with this problem. In a 1976 survey, only 20 treatment programs for sex offenders in the United States could be identified (Brecher, 1978). Of those, only one was developed to deal exclusively with perpetrators of child sexual abuse.[1] Similarly, in 1978 the National Center on Child Abuse and Neglect (NCCAN) estimated that there were no more than a dozen programs specifically designed to treat intra-family child sexual abuse. By 1981, NCCAN had identified more than 300 such programs nation-wide which contain specialized components to deal with various aspects of this problem.[2] Although many of these programs have benefited from increased federal and state funding, most survive on a year-to-year basis with a combination of public and private resources and client fees for service. Many are struggling for survival in the face of rapidly increasing caseloads[3] and diminishing public funds.

This paper examines the range of child sexual abuse programs which provide treatment services in non-residential, community settings. Specialized programs for abusers in prison or mental institutions are not reviewed. Its primary focus is on the management of intrafamily child sexual abuse cases, although it should be recognized that the programs discussed include many over-lapping avenues of comparison and do not reflect the kind of "pure" program models that can be neatly or exclusively categorized. This overview offers some ways of considering the various program types, although it does not provide descriptions of specific programs or attempt to compare them individually. It focuses on the types of treatment systems that specialized programs have helped to establish in their communities, since it is the development of these comprehensive systems that sets them apart from more traditional handling of child sexual abuse cases.

Background Issues

By way of background, it is useful to look briefly at some of the systemic problems and dilemmas associated with child sexual abuse that have spawned the development of such a range of specialized programs. A fundamental dilemma centers around professional and societal ambivalence about whether child sexual abuse should be regarded as a crime, a form of mental illness, or (particularly in cases of incest), as a major symptom of broader family dysfunction. The view or composite of views that one has toward child sexual abuse can constitute a major determinant in how it is dealt with in any given system. The difficulties inherent in such concepts as "prosecuting an illness," "treating a crime," or applying both strategies to a "family problem" are currently being grappled with by programs throughout the country. The ways in which these various orientations are reflected in program models will be discussed later in this paper. The following issues provide a synopsis of the major problems and procedural barriers which communities have had to face in developing various program alternatives.

Low Likelihood of Successful Prosecution

Even if one has no philosophical conflict about prosecuting child sexual abuse in the same manner as any other violation of criminal law, traditional prosecution of these cases has shown itself to be a frustrating and largely unsuccessful endeavor if the desired outcomes are conviction and lengthy incarceration. Since prosecutors are reluctant to go to court with cases that are unlikely to result in convictions (particularly when they require an inordinate amount of preparation time), cases involving child sexual abuse, especially where the perpetrator is a family member, often do not reach criminal court at all.[4] This is compounded by the generally accepted fact that most cases never even come to the attention of authorities.

The extreme difficulty in prosecuting child sexual abuse cases utilizing traditional legal procedures is largely because they are rarely accompanied by the kinds of evidence necessary to establish proof of guilt beyond a reasonable doubt. Evidentiary limitations include: lack of forensic evidence of sexual activity or physical violence; time lapse between the abuse and its discovery; lack of corroborative eye witnesses; reluctance of family members and friends to press charges or testify in court; and pressure on children to retract their statements due to fears of family disintegration. These are compounded by the belief that children do not make credible witnesses due to their limited cognitive and verbal abilities and alleged suggestibility, and the fact that accused abusers are unmotivated to plead guilty when alternatives to incarceration are few or the chances of acquittal are high.

In many instances, a prosecutor's case hinges solely on the word of a young child against the word of an adult—often a very credible adult with a good employment record, no prior arrests, apparent parental or civic concern for children and a good defense attorney. It is no wonder that so many child sexual abuse cases result in reduced pleas with no real consequences for perpetrators, dropped charges, or no charges at all (Bulkley, 1981a; Sgroi, 1978).

Increased Trauma from the "Helping" System

Perhaps the greatest incentive to the development of specialized approaches to this problem comes from the collective observations of concerned professionals that the trauma experienced by child victims and their families can be substantially compounded by duplicative and insensitive interventions on the part of criminal justice and child protective systems (Berliner and Stevens, 1980; Giarretto, 1976; MacFarlane, 1978).

The trouble with traditional approaches to legal intervention in these cases is that they inevitably require a singular focus on obtaining the kinds of physical or corroborative evidence necessary to prove a case in court. The various procedures to which a child may be subjected by the justice system have been documented elsewhere in the literature (Berliner and Stevens, 1980; Giarretto, 1976; MacFarlane, 1978). They include: multiple detailed interrogation by law enforcement, medical and social service personnel; gynecological examinations that may include sedation or the use of restraints; subjection to polygraph tests and hypnosis; the appearance of uniformed police in the home or at school; testimony and cross-examination at a preliminary hearing, grand jury or open trial; involuntary separation from family; and others.

The brunt of this system-induced trauma can be attributed to several factors that are currently being addressed by most programs: (1) lack of coordination and cooperation among the systems and professionals involved in these cases; (2) lack of skill and sensitivity in dealing with child victims; (3) little allowance, particularly in the criminal justice system, for the special vulnerabilities of child witnesses; and (4) lack of options and flexibility in dealing with an offense whose victims and perpetrators often have very complex and mixed feelings about each other.

Limited Jurisdiction and Resources of Child Protection Agencies

Services provided by child protective service agencies (CPS) and ordered by juvenile courts focus on protection of children and help for families, rather than on punishment of abusers. In contrast to the criminal court, juvenile court proceedings generally are regarded as less traumatic for children (Bulkley and Davidson, 1981), and may be less threatening to parents who sometimes are more likely to cooperate with an agency's treatment plan when they are not facing criminal prosecution. However, while CPS agencies and the juvenile court can order and provide needed supervision and services to a child and family, they do not have direct control over the perpetrators of abuse. This can have immediate consequences for a child since, in the absence of the authority to order abusers out of their homes, the placement of victims (and sometimes their siblings) in foster homes is often regarded as the only means of assuring their protection. Such a move often leaves children feeling punished and guilty for the abuse or for its discovery.

Even without the limitations of out-of-home placements, CPS agencies often are ill-equipped to provide comprehensive treatment for this problem. In a 1980 study of sexual abuse case handling in public social agencies in the southeast (N = 1,045), it was found that CPS workers generally viewed their jobs as consisting of investigation and diagnosis, and that the majority delegated the reponsibility for providing treatment to other resources. In addition, although the overwhelming majority of workers indicated that they felt unprepared to offer treatment, less than 50% wanted the responsibility for it—even is adequate specialized training was made available to them (Johnson, 1981). The fact that most CPS workers lack the specialized skills, educational backgrounds, time, or even the mandate to provide long-term treatment for sexually abusive families,[5] led a variety of other community agencies to take the lead in developing the specialized resources needed.

Difficulty in Keeping Families in Treatment

Individual therapeutic resources for child sexual abusers existed in most communities long before most specialized treatment programs came into existence. Special court arrangements, which are still available in many places, often involved agreements between defense and prosecuting attorneys (with the recommendations of private psychiatrists), that resulted in guilty pleas with treatment on an outpatient basis as a condition of probation. The problems with this solution, even if mandated by the court, include the following: (1) accountability for such arrangements is generally low, as is the long-term follow-through in many cases; (2) individual psychotherapists, regardless of their educational credentials, usually have little expertise in treating this problem due to limited experience and the lack of specialized training in the curricula of professional schools; (3) traditional, one-hour-a-week, non-directive or insight-oriented modes of psychotherapy have not proven to be very effective with this problem when offered in the absence of other types of intervention (Giarretto, 1978); (4) the child and other family members who may have played various roles in the abusive situation or who are suffering as a consequence of it, often are not the recipients of any remedial services themselves; (5) the confidential nature of the private patient-therapist relationship can serve to reinforce the secrecy and collusion that are inherent aspects of this form of abuse; and, finally (6) when there is no meaningful outside supervision, enforcement of boundaries or feedback mechanism (as in simultaneous treatment of the victim and other parent), or when the abuser remains in the home, the abuse may well continue while the abuser is "engaged" in treatment.

Of all the drawbacks to the singular, individualistic "solution" to child sexual abuse, perhaps the most obvious problem was, and remains, the extreme difficulty in engaging and keeping child sexual abusers in treatment. Whether the fault lies primarily with the limitations of traditional treatment methods, the inadequate skills of many therapists, the fear on the part of abusers of further shame or retribution, their inherent denial, defensiveness and resistance to acknowledging that they have this problem, or the unavoidable stigma associated with it, the problem remains that child sexual abusers are not a client population that willingly comes to or readily stays engaged in traditional psychotherapy.

Major Program Types

The most difficult aspect of any attempt to analyze or compare treatment systems is the development of a conceptual framework by which they can be examined in an organized manner. This is especially true when virtually none of the program categories are mutually exclusive, and nearly every effort at generalization can be punctuated by its exception. Bearing this in mind, the following observations are offered as a first attempt at formulating a conceptual scheme for describing various programmatic approaches to the treatment of child sexual abuse.

Because child sexual abuse is contained in both criminal statutes and child abuse reporting laws, an obvious avenue of program comparison is the relationship of treatment programs to existing criminal justice and child protective systems. Working relationships between legal and therapeutic systems are characteristically complex and delicate in nature, and the example of child sexual abuse programs is no exception. They range from seeking the active involvement of the criminal justice system, often incorporating the coercive authority of the legal system into their treatment philosophies and program procedures, to the deliberate shunning of legal coercion and what they view to be the stigmatizing emphasis on criminality which is seen as antithetical to a therapeutic process.

The factors that determine a program's relationship with pre-existing systems of authority are often multi-dimensional and deserve more discussion than space will permit. However briefly, they include: (1) predominant philosophical orientations toward child sexual abuse (that is, whether it is perceived as a crime, illness or family problem can account for different perceptions in the kinds of legal authority and remedies needed); (2) constitutional, statutory, or procedural limitations in state and federal laws (for example, mandatory sentences for certain sex crimes may preclude "therapeutic" dispositions; or pre-trial diversion may not be

authorized by state statute); (3) a program's ability and the legal
system's responsiveness to change pre-existing attitudes or methods
of dealing with these cases; (4) availability of alternative resources
or skilled personnel; and (5) the existence of individuals in positions of authority who share the belief systems necessary to initiate
a program in the community. Whatever the philosophies or constraints that circumscribe the relationships between various programs and the power bases in their communities, these relationships play an important part in shaping the character and operation
of specialized treatment systems. Recognizing the artificial nature
of any simplified program classification, the following represents an
attempt to describe child sexual abuse treatment programs within
the framework of a few general categories.

The Victim Advocacy Model: Softening the Process

This approach is characterized by a strongly victim-centered orientation and by the belief that child sexual abuse is a crime which
requires the visible condemnation by society in the form of strong
legal sanctions and the active involvement of the criminal justice
system. It often includes the assumption that the prosecution and
punishment of rape and sexual assault should not be determined by
the age of the victim or by the relationship to the abuser. Such an
approach often incorporates the belief that going forward with
prosecution is one way of demonstrating to children that society will
protect them, and that their rights and welfare are valued. Whether
a program model has the stated goal of achieving court-ordered
treatment for abusers or whether it advocates for sanctions in addition to rehabilitation, it may operate under the premise that the
process of prosecution or criminal justice intervention has a positive
value in itself; that legal proceedings are not only necessary, but
desirable when conducted in ways that are sensitive to the needs and
limitations of victims.

Many child sexual abuse programs in this category have evolved
from victim-witness program models or from the many excellent
rape crisis centers around the country. Their efforts generally are
not so much aimed at changing or improving the criminal justice
system as a whole, but at ameliorating those procedures or aspects
of the system that can be detrimental to children or that result in
nothing being done on their behalf. Their services, which are fo-

cused almost exclusively on child victims, usually involve case advocacy in helping the child and family negotiate the system, emergency assistance, legal consultation, and short-term counselling. Some hospitals and CPS agencies, which may call themselves treatment programs, would more appropriately fall into this category of advocacy programs, since what they offer are predominantly diagnostic services, medical or psychological evaluation, advocacy, and crisis intervention.

One of the disadvantages of advocating for case resolution within the existing criminal justice system in order to demonstrate to children that they are valued and believed, is the risk that dropped charges, dismissal of cases or findings of not guilty may have the effect of proving the exact opposite to children. Children may even end up feeling punished for participating in the process if they must be placed in foster care because a suspected abuser will be returned to the home following acquittal in criminal court.

Despite the drawbacks of choosing to operate within a system whose outcomes are influenced by factors beyond their control, the advocacy types of programs have done much to support child victims of sexual abuse and to raise the consciousness of their communities regarding the needs of sexual abuse victims. Although they have thereby changed the process by changing attitudes, the majority of their efforts are targeted toward improving the treatment of children on a case-by-case basis. Traditional systems may not be observably different (in terms of any formal changes in the policies or procedures of community agencies) as a result of the efforts of programs in this category, but they have become appreciably more sensitive in their dealings with children (Bulkley and Davidson, 1981).

The Improvement Model: Embracing but Humanizing the System

Analogous to the victim advocacy model, the central focus of the improvement model is the child victim. However, programs under this model have had a greater impact upon the criminal justice system by developing new procedures for bringing about more sensitive intervention as well as successful prosecutions. Many of these programs have invested an impressive amount of time and effort in devising multidisciplinary techniques for improving and humanizing the investigation and prosecution of child sexual abuse cases.[6]

Under this model, the juvenile court may not be utilized but protection orders may be issued by the criminal court to insure the child's safety. This often allows the child to remain in the home with the non-abusing parent, while the abuser leaves the home, either temporarily or permanently.

As with the victim advocacy model, programs in this category strongly advocate and encourage the use of criminal prosecution, when sensitively handled, both as a symbolic action to the child and society, and as a method of obtaining dispositions involving court-ordered treatment services for the abuser. These programs generally do not endorse prosecuting the crime of child sexual abuse simply because it is a crime. Nor do they support incarceration of abusers in all cases, especially in incest cases. The results achieved under this model involve two premises. First, successful prosecutions are more likely when the legal system is more sensitive to the child and more knowledgeable regarding child development and dynamics of sexual abuse. Likewise, it is argued, a higher prosecution rate tends to lead to more guilty pleas, resulting in less trauma to the child (since fewer cases go through the entire trial process), as well as an opportunity to provide treatment for the abuser in exchange for his guilty plea.

A successful prosecution rate has largely been accomplished through the reform of laws and prosecutorial practices and policies, with emphasis on maximizing the credibility of the child victim as a witness (*Progress Report,* 1979). Because few cases are deemed "unprosecutable," and because treatment programs and prosecutor's offices have worked closely together in developing new approaches and strategies for improving the quality of prosecution, cases are more often settled.[7] Moreover, through the process of plea negotiation, additional benefits are derived, such as: abusers who plead guilty generally receive treatment as a condition of a sentence of probation or work-release; abusers often are able to continue supporting their families by maintaining their employment; and victims and other family members are spared the ordeal and expense of going to trial.

Since many of these programs began with a strict victim-orientation, most did not originally develop the goal of providing treatment for the abuser. However, treatment for abusers has evolved into an important component of many programs in this model, whether it is provided by the same program as is treating the victim, or by referral to other community resources. Treatment for abusers is generally seen as a sentencing alternative to incarceration after an abuser has been convicted. Indeed, according to these programs, the idea that abusers will seek help voluntarily is an anathema which involves setting up mental health practitioners as the monitors and enforcers of compliance with the rules of society and conditions of treatment. Moreover, unlike the System Modification Model described later, the criminal justice system is considered to be more than simply an incentive or leverage to secure a defendant's admission into treatment. Rather, it is thought of as an equal, if not dominant partner in its relationship with the treatment program in determining the disposition and ongoing supervision of cases. As a result, although treatment providers may feel somewhat absolved of having to "police" the prior or ongoing behavior of their clients, they usually must abdicate a certain amount of control over case outcomes (especially during the court process) to a more powerful and usually less therapeutically-oriented system.

The System Modification Model: Creating Systemic Changes in Legal Intervention

Under this model there are a variety of approaches which have involved a fundamental rethinking of traditional methods of handling intrafamily child sexual abuse cases in both the criminal and juvenile courts. Major re-structuring of legal procedures, processes and dispositions have occurred in a number of jurisdictions. There are several variations on the manner in which traditional legal action has been altered under this model, although these varied approaches also share a number of common philosophies and goals. Before discussing specific types of approaches, these shared premises merit examination.

Perhaps the most common thread reflected in this model is the paramount concern for reducing the impact and trauma of the legal process upon the child and family by altering existing systems in ways that will cause them to be more compatible with that goal. However, of nearly equal importance is the belief that incarceration for most intrafamily abusers is of little or no benefit to the child, family or society (Giarretto, 1976; MacFarlane, 1978). Programs in this model do not advocate for decriminalization of intrafamily sex offenses against children. Rather, the criminal justice system is considered crucial in motivating or providing an authoritative incentive for abusers and families to participate in treatment (Giarretto, 1976; Bulkley, 1981b). Thus, criminal court action in intrafamily cases is not viewed as serving the traditional purpose of punishment or retribution, but is thought of as a means for achieving rehabilitation. The combination of criminal justice and therapeutic dispositions are believed to provide a deterrent to future sexual abuse by the perpetrator as well as by other potential abusers.

Another premise shared by most legal systems and treatment programs under this as well as other models, is the belief that the problem of intrafamily child sexual abuse requires a family treatment approach (Bulkley, 1981b). This does not mean that a programs's primary goal is to "save" families as they exist at the time of reporting, but that all family members need treatment, both separately and together, to deal with the problems that have affected them all. This goal, which is common to most of these treatment approaches, involves helping family members to understand the options that are available to them, and to develop the insight and self-awareness necessary to make responsible and beneficial decisions about their futures—whether that means staying together or separating. Where it is in the best interests of the child, efforts are made to help families who wish to be re-united to work toward that end. Thus, as a general rule, the police, prosecutor and CPS worker refer cases to a specialized sexual abuse treatment program (which may exist as a separate component within any of their own agencies) which provides services to the entire family. Specialized incest programs exist under other models as well, although it is a more common feature of this model.

With the exception of the third subcategory to be discussed, most programs within this model often do not involve juvenile court action. Thus, another common characteristic is that juvenile court petitions may not be filed where criminal court actions have been initiated and where the non-abusive parent is able to care for and protect the child and is willing to participate in treatment.

This idea seems to reflect an unexpected trend in the reform of the legal system's involvement in these cases. The use of the legal system to protect abused children traditionally has been the province of the juvenile court. However, programs under this model seem to regard the juvenile court as having the potential to cause greater harm to the child due to the risk of unnecessary removal from the home. It is the criminal court that is seen as the primary vehicle for protecting the child, since it can order the abuser out of the home or insure that he has no contact with the child or other family members for a specified period of time. This permits the child to remain with the non-abusive parent. The juvenile court does continue to be utilized, however, where leverage is needed over non-abusing parents who have ambivalent feelings about the abuser and the child, or to insure that they will seek treatment for themselves, as well as for their children (Bulkley and Davidson, 1981).

As noted earlier, the innovative approaches that may be categorized under this model vary in terms of the changes they have brought about within the legal system. These approaches essentially fall into three prototype sub-categories: (1) *post-conviction, therapeutic sentencing* which involves providing treatment as a condition of disposition.[8] This approach is characterized by innovative police techniques for securing confessions, immediate treatment for all family members—often involving self-help groups—and infrequent prison sentences. If incarcerated, most abusers serve time in local county jails under work-furlough programs which allow them to retain their jobs and attend treatment sessions. Goals include avoiding family involvement in criminal trials by obtaining guilty pleas, and engaging the abuser in treatment soon after disclosure of the abuse; (2) *pre-trial diversion* involves diverting a defendant from the criminal process prior to trial in exchange for his performance of specified obligations—most notably, successful completion of a treatment program, after which the case is usually dismissed.[9] Advocates of diversion claim that one advantage over post-conviction treatment is the abuser's motivation to avoid a criminal record. At the same time, he remains under the control of the criminal justice system, fully subject to prosecution and criminal sanctions if the terms of the diversion agreement are violated (Bulkley, 1981b; De Grazia, 1974; Nimmer, 1974; *Performance Standards*, 1978); and (3) *coordinated criminal and juvenile court processing* which involves primary jurisdiction in the juvenile court where efforts are made to secure agreements from the abuser and family to obtain treatment in exchange for deferring criminal prosecution (Bulkley, 1981b). This approach avoids instituting two separate proceedings, and, if settled in juvenile court, avoids exposing children to the criminal court process. Criminal prosecution is subsequently initiated if the agreement is violated.

The Independent Model: Serving as a Resource, Not a Participant

Rather than taking a stand for or against criminal or juvenile court involvement in cases of sexual abuse, there are some treatment programs that appear to operate essentially independently of the legal and political systems in their communities. Some of them are quite comprehensive in terms of the variety of services they offer to victims, abusers, or all family members. They seem to operate on the premise that child sexual abuse is an illness or a family problem which requires and deserves specialized therapeutic resources regardless of what may be being done about the problem within the legal system. Such programs are not necessarily characterized by their treatment orientations; some follow an illness or psychiatric model and emphasize that sexual abuse is a disease, while others take the more social casework or family systems approach of attempting to intervene on several levels to re-program dysfunctional and abusive family dynamics. Similarly, they may utilize very different treatment methods, such as psychiatric counseling, self-help groups, sex therapy, and various educational techniques.

Programs in this category are not easy to classify within a systems framework except to say that they generally did not become involved in the treatment business as a result of strong advocacy, political, or reformist motivations, and they tend to stay out of those arenas whenever possible. However, because of the multidisciplinary nature of child sexual abuse, it is often not possible for these or any treatment programs to remain totally apart from the legal systems in their communities. Even so, the periodic involvement of these types of programs with criminal and juvenile justice systems appears to occur as a matter of individual case necessity, rather than by design.

Inadvertent program involvement with outside legal systems is more likely to occur when: (1) a program's client is facing criminal charges or sentencing and needs a professional recommendation as to his treatability; (2) when there is an issue of child protection or alternative placement involving a family in treatment; or (3) when a program is requested by the court to provide evaluations or expert opinions concerning specific cases before the court. Programs that endeavor to remain uninvolved with systems of authority in their communities might be seen as disadvantaged through their abdication of an opportunity to influence those systems that can so strongly affect their clients. Nonetheless, they are serious in their efforts to develop better treatment methods, and they seem resolved in maintaining that focus.

The System Alternative Model: Treatment Without Law Enforcement

Programs in this category are, in many respects, like those described in the Independent Model, except that they go beyond a desire to remain apart from the legal system's involvement in incest cases by taking a philosophical position against the deliberate use of the criminal, as well as juvenile court, either to punish or to enforce treatment orders. While their position has evolved into a political one, given the investment of the large segment of society and community agencies which view this problem primarily as a crime, their treatment orientation is totally a therapeutic one aimed at the whole family. Family members are not regarded as "offenders" or defendants in an adversarial situation, but as individuals with illnesses or dysfunctional behavior patterns which require therapeutic intervention.

Advocates of this approach acknowledge the extreme difficulty of keeping abusers and other family members engaged in treatment, but they do not regard court orders or legal coercion as a means of solving that problem. Rather, the justice system is seen as an artificial mechanism for commanding clients' physical presence at therapy sessions. The issue is not simply one of opposition to the use of the justice system to "motivate" family members or to enforce treatment orders. An underlying premise for this model involves the conviction that, if intervention is going to be truly psychotherapeutic, any conditions which interfere with that process must be identified and eliminated or avoided. The conditions necessary for establishing a treatment alliance or conducting psychotherapy are not seen as being subject to the power of a court mandate or the influence of plea bargains. This model considers use of the criminal court to order or "persuade" an abuser to enter a treatment program as antithetical to the concept of psychotherapeutic treatment, which is seen as premised on personal motivation and the need or desire to change destructive behaviors and attitudes. Similarly, the therapeutic requirement of sharing highly personal data under confidential circumstances in the presence of voluntary and willing consent are not only central to this approach, but are seen as threatened by models which represent a marriage between law enforcement and the "helping professions" (Greenberg, 1979).

A blurring of professional roles is seen, under this model, as one consequence of cooperation with the criminal justice system: the concern is that, caseworkers and therapists who work within coercive therapy models inadvertently are becoming an arm of the legal system. A conflict of interest is perceived when diagnostic interviews become synonymous with the process of evidence gathering, or when "confidential" information, shared during the early stages of therapy, is used to determine the legal status or future freedom of clients. Programs under other models strongly favor the involvement of the criminal justice system as a means of separating the powers of law enforcement from the efforts of treatment providers, while advocates of this model view such involvement as the very vehicle by which such conflict of interest occurs.

Like other approaches, this model primarily focuses on protecting the child victim, preventing further harm, and ameliorating the consequences of the abuse. Of equal importance, however, is a concern and commitment to the welfare of all members of the family, and to the preservation of family life whenever possible and in the best interests of family members. This commitment to best interests of individual clients includes the preservation of individual privacy, confidentiality and trust within a therapeutic relationship. Criminal justice and mental health systems are not regarded as mutual or even compatible in terms of purpose, priorities or procedures. When compromises that permit such coexistence are made by introducing non-therapeutic procedures into the mental health arena, the compromises are seen as having been made on the side of legal systems (Greenberg, 1979).

As with some other models, the use of authority is an important issue in this approach. Coercive power or "external" authority based upon the threat of punishment is regarded as an unacceptable substitute for the inherent authority that is present in a treatment alliance based upon genuine concern for the welfare of the individual. Such an alliance is not established immediately, is influenced by the circumstances under which treatment is initiated, and is seen as largely dependent upon the skills, knowledge and expertise of the treatment provider. One premise of programs which rely primarily on this type of "professional," rather than "institutional" authority to overcome resistance and bring about intentional behavior and attitudinal changes, is that the nature and duration of such changes will be different, depending on the nature of clients' motivation and the application of power and authority within therapeutic relationships. At this point in time, the data do not exist that would allow the comparison of treatment approaches or outcomes based upon the use of various forms of authority.

Programs in this model generally are closely allied with (or sometimes contained within) public child protective systems. Programs rely on them as a source of referrals (thereby reducing the need to act as the reporting source except in cases of repeated abuse), and serve as the therapeutic back-up system and treatment resources to the investigative process of the CPS agency. Under this model, the separation of family members, including the placement of children, may occur in order to protect a child from future abuse or to reduce crises, but it is not done as a matter of program policy, legal safeguards, or personal reaction. Separation, whether it is based on a recommendation to juvenile court or on the program's use of its own authority to insist that a parent leave the home (a non-legal practice which has resulted in surprising degrees of compliance in other program models as well) occurs within the context of what will best serve the initiation and continuation of a treatment alliance. Such decisions are based solely on their therapeutic indications which include the child's safety (Greenberg, 1979). This model is controversial due to its divisionary stance from both the criminal and juvenile courts, and its feasibility is somewhat uncertain in states which require mandatory reporting of first offense child sexual abuse cases to police or prosecutors. Nonetheless, it represents an attempt to accomplish (without legal coercion) most of the same goals as those programs that work within the justice system.

Reflections on an Emerging Trend: The "Godfather Offer"

One approach to dealing with intrafamily child sexual abuse cases is becoming such a dominant trend in the development of many systems that it merits examination by itself. Since this approach constitutes a technique for accomplishing the provision of treatment services, and is utilized by so many different types of programs, it is difficult to classify within any one model.

Basically, the approach involves offering a defendant the opportunity to avoid criminal prosecution, harsh penalties or other sanc-

tions in exchange for certain concessions, usually involving his acknowledgement of the abuse, cooperation with treatment, and other
pre-established criteria. In jurisdictions which provide treatment following conviction, the offer may be used in obtaining confessions or
guilty pleas. Such offers generally involve anticipated outcomes or
mutually hoped-for consequences of certain actions, rather than a
promise of specific results (that is, "90% of the people who cooperate receive this instead of that"). Or, in pre-trial diversion programs, the offer may be made by the prosecutor in the form of a
formal pledge or specific contractual arrangement to defer prosecution (that is, "if you do these things, we will guarantee those
things").

In cases of child sexual abuse, the offer is basically a bartering of
things that are usually highly desired on all sides. Depending on the
specific conditions of such an exchange, the benefits can include: (1)
for the criminal justice system, a guilty plea or avoidance of the time
and expense of litigation; (2) for a treatment program, the likelihood that, because of the continuing threat of punishment or prosecution, the abuser will not drop out of treatment; (3) for a victim,
the avoidance of having to testify against a parent or having to feel
responsible for the abuser's punishment; (4) for other family members, the opportunity to avoid the expense and stigma of a public
trial, and to receive therapy to work through dysfunctional behaviors, even if separation is desired; and (5) for the abuser, a means of
avoiding prison or a criminal record, as well as the loss of employment and status. As in the movie, *The Godfather,* it is an offer
which, if not impossible, is at least very difficult for an accused
abuser to refuse when faced with a felony charge of incest or child
sexual assault.

A number of legal and treatment issues arise from the use of this
approach. From a legal perspective, the "Godfather Offer" is a
device for obtaining a confession, a guilty plea, or a defendant's
participation in pretrial diversion. Programs must use caution in
order to insure that a guilty plea or agreement to participate in a
diversion program is legally valid; that is, it must be voluntary and
knowing (Newman, 1966). Likewise, confessions must be voluntary;
if they are obtained by psychological coercion, they are considered
involuntary, regardless of their actual truth or falsity.[10] In order to
satisfy the voluntariness requirement, the defendant must understand the nature of the charges, the requirements of the program or

conditions of a plea, the consequences if he violates these requirements, and his waiver of various rights. A defendant's access to an
attorney who is familiar with the program is one way of assuring
that his choice is a knowing one.

With regard to the efficacy of treatment, there is some question
about whether any decision by an accused to confess, plead guilty or
enter into a diversion agreement can, in fact, be voluntary. It is
unlikely that a suspect facing criminal charges or prison decides to
acknowledge responsibility for sexual abuse solely because he is
repentant. For the most part, such decisions are made because of
fear of punishment or to avoid the legal process; through acceptance
of a special offer, defendants can avoid or limit pain (Rosett and
Cressey, 1976). This is not meant to imply that abusers and their
families who enter treatment programs under such conditions cannot benefit from or become engaged in a treatment process. Many
treatment providers will attest to the positive changes they have
seen in what, initially, were resistant and manipulative clients seeking to avoid criminal court. Nonetheless, programs are becoming
cognizant of the fact that when the legal system, rather than the
abuser's personal desire to change is the primary, if not exclusive,
initial motivation to participate in therapy, treatment methods and
expectations must be tailored accordingly.

Factors That Influence Program Approaches

There are many variables other than programs' relationships with
criminal and juvenile justice systems that have affected their development, and many other ways of comparing them. For example,
while the auspice agency or host organization of a particular program may have a strong influence on its direction and parameters,
very different types of programs exist within similar settings. While
hospital-based programs often maintain a strong focus on the medical and forensic aspects of cases, to assume that they all offer primarily diagnostic and crisis intervention services would be a disservice
to a number of very comprehensive hospital-based programs.[11] Similarly, although many public child protection agencies primarily in-
vestigate reports and provide short-term, individual counseling,
some CPS agencies are providing a full range of services on a long-
term basis.[12] Further, it is often criminal justice agencies, working in
conjunction with treatment specialists, that are leading the way in

developing systems which divert abusers out of the usual process of criminal prosecution and into treatment.[13]

While the focus or intended focus of services, (e.g., types of clients) has been an influential factor in program development, it has become an increasingly less useful measure of comparison as programs begin to re-examine their intake criteria or the actual populations they are serving. Few have remained "pure" with regard to a strongly defined treatment population. Although the intake criteria of programs often include such prohibitions as: no physical violence associated with the sexual abuse, no prior criminal record, no substance abuse, and no evidence of sexual abuse of children outside the family, many programs have discovered all of these problems in families once they are in treatment. Some are finding that the existence of physical child abuse, spouse abuse, alcoholism, or extrafamilial pedophilia have not always precluded the responsiveness of these families to treatment. As a result, most programs have begun developing the resources necessary to work with increasingly diverse types of client problems.

It is particularly significant that even those programs whose original intention was to serve either families that were not involved with the criminal justice system or families that were directly tied to it through some formal procedure, are currently serving families in both categories.[14] It seems apparent that, while programs are attempting to define their treatment populations in ways which are narrow enough to test particular approaches with clients whom they believe are likely to be successful, many of them also are committed to working with clients who respond to treatment, regardless of how well they may fit the specified criteria.

Finally, a factor that is important but often overlooked is the influence of the program developers themselves. Child sexual abuse programs have been strongly influenced by a diverse number of unique and committed individuals, rather than by any one profession. Many programs exist today because of the efforts and perseverance of one or two people. These early pioneers in the field carved out program models from what often were destructive or indifferent systems, and many initially faced hostile or skeptical community reactions. They learned from their clients, from the efforts of other community agencies, and from their own mistakes, many of the things that we collectively know today.

The founders of successful programs have shown that the political process of program development is as important as the best of intentions, and most have utilized as much influence in their communities as they could muster. Their recognition of the need to intervene at systems as well as individual levels, coupled with their own philosophical assumptions about this problem, have contributed greatly to the conceptualization of current program models. As treatment methods and results are evaluated and better documented, it is anticipated that service providers in this field will be able to learn as much from each other as from their own efforts.

Conclusion

While it is clear that specialized programs for treating child sexual abuse share many common concerns, goals, legal barriers and treatment methods, it is also readily apparent that substantial philosophical and programmatic differences exist among them. Although the extreme range of existing approaches may be frustrating to policy makers and confusing to program developers who search for the "best" model to replicate, such diversity is not wholly undesirable, given our current limited knowledge and understanding of the nature, causes and effects of child sexual abuse and its treatment.

Encouraging as it has been to see the growth of specialized resources to deal with this difficult problem over the past decade, the lack of equivalent focus and funding for program evaluations and assessment of treatment outcomes has left the field with little empirical data to compare the results of various types of intervention. Federal and state funding sources, like treatment providers themselves, focused early efforts on the immediate need to develop specialized treatment programs and provide specific training for professionals in the field of child protection. The anticipation that funding for evaluation and research would follow early treatment efforts, however, grows increasingly dim as federal and state fiscal priorities rapidly shift in a direction away from any involvement in categorical service programs. Even federal evaluation contracts, funded in conjunction with sexual abuse demonstration efforts, have been hampered by government unwillingness to collect data that are considered to be "highly sensitive" in nature.

Fortunately, an increasing number of treatment programs throughout the country have begun conducting their own research and program evaluations. Over the next few years these efforts should produce much more empirical evidence of program effectiveness than the mostly descriptive information and clinical case observations that characterize much of the professional literature currently available. Still needed, however, is the capability of comparing the outcomes of various program models as well as the actual treatment methods utilized. Comparative research of this kind is costly and time-consuming but necessary if we are to move beyond the "innovative" phase of program development. To abandon efforts to acquire the evidence of the impressive results that have been observed and reported by the professionals and clients associated with some of these programs, would be to diminish many of the efforts and resources that have gone to create them.

The number and array of specialized program approaches can be viewed as a positive sign of the commitment and energy in this field. In most cases, they represent attempts to safeguard systems and procedures that contain within them the potential to harm as well as help. However, the diversity among programs and the obvious investment of individuals in their own program models calls for an increasing need to guard against polarization within the still relatively small community of professionals concerned with this problem. There is not enough comparative evidence at this point in time to warrant competition or territorialism around treasured approaches, and it will only serve to distract attention from the larger problem of shifting domestic priorities. It is ironic that, at a time when public support and resources are rapidly dwindling, we have learned enough to realize the great need for more knowledge, training and research. When budgets shrink, training and program specialization are seen as luxuries. However, a future of limited resources should not justify the loss of what has been gained over the past decade in combatting this problem. If prevention and treatment of child sexual abuse becomes luxuries we cannot afford, we shall continue to pay an immeasurable human cost.

NOTES

1. The Child Sexual Abuse Treatment Program; Juvenile Probation Department, San Jose, California.
2. Unpublished program list compiled by Kee MacFarlane, NCCAN, 1980.
3. Reported cases of child sexual abuse have nearly doubled every year since 1976 when the American Humane Association began collecting national statistics on reported cases under a grant from the National Center on Child Abuse and Neglect.

4. For example, statistics compiled by Children's Hospital National Medical Center in Washington, D.C. reveal that, from February, 1978 through November, 1980, roughly 60% of reported child sexual abuse cases were dismissed prior to the filing of criminal charges, and almost one-third of the charges filed were also dismissed. Recent data from Sexual Assault Services in Hennepin County, Minnesota indicate that, in almost half of the reported child sexual abuse cases, charges are not filed (Bulkley, 1981b).

5. This is not meant to imply that CPS agencies are unsuited or incapable of becoming focal points for specialized programs (see note #13 *infra*), only that it is not usually accomplished without specific training, procedures or a mandate.

6. Notably, the Sexual Assault Center of Harborview Medical Center, Seattle, Washington.

7. In jurisdictions such as Hennepin County, Minnesota, Baltimore, Maryland, and Seattle, Washington, which have developed such approaches, the percentage of guilty pleas ranges from 75% to 100%.

8. Pioneered by the Child Sexual Abuse Treatment Program in San Jose, California.

9. Notable examples are the Johnson County Child Sexual Abuse Treatment Program, Johnson County Mental Health Center, in Olathe, Kansas, and the Sacramento Child Sexual Abuse Treatment Program in Sacramento, California.

10. See *Jordan v. People,* 419 P. 2d 656, 660 (Colo. 1966), in which a confession of an incest offender was upheld as voluntary. See also *State v. Miller,* 388 A. 2d 218 (N.J. 1978), which stated that the use by police of a "psychologically-oriented" technique in questioning is not inherently coercive.

11. For example, Harborview Medical Center in Seattle, Washington; Fairview Southdale Hospital in Edina, Minnesota; Tufts Medical Center in Boston, Massachusetts.

12. For example, Child Protective Services programs in: Rockville, Maryland; Colorado Springs, Colorado; Albuquerque, New Mexico; Tucson, Arizona; Greenville, South Carolina, Virginia Beach, Virginia, and many others.

13. Examples include: Sacramento, California, Olathe, Kansas, Baltimore, Maryland, Des Moines, Iowa and others.

14. Personal communication between Kee MacFarlane and directors at: Child and Family Services, Knoxville, Tennessee; CAUSES, Chicago, Illinois; Harborview Medical Center, Seattle, Washington; Institute for the Community as Extended Family, San Jose, California; and Sacramento Child Sexual Abuse Treatment Program, Sacramento, California.

REFERENCES

Berliner, L. and Stevens, D. "Advocating for the Sexually Abused Child in the Criminal Justice System," in *Sexual Abuse of Children: Selected Readings,* eds. MacFarlane, K., Jones, B., and Jenstrom, L., National Center on Child Abuse and Neglect, Govt. Printing Office, November, 1980, pp. 47–50, Washington, D.C.

Brecher, E. *Treatment Programs for Sex Offenders.* National Institute for Law Enforcement and Criminal Justice, Law Enforcement Assistance Administration, U.S. Department of Justice, Government Printing Office, January, 1978, Washington, D.C.

Bulkley, J. *Child Sexual Abuse and the Law.* National Legal Resource Center for Child Advocacy and Protection, American Bar Association, July, 1981a, Washington, D.C.

Bulkley, J. *Innovations in the Prosecution of Child Sexual Abuse Cases.* National Legal Resource Center for Child Advocacy and Protection, American Bar Association, November, 1981b, Washington, D.C.

Bulkley, J. and Davidson, H. *Child Sexual Abuse—Legal Issues and Approaches.* National Legal Resource Center for Child Advocacy and Protection, American Bar Association, Rev. Ed., August, 1981, Washington, D.C.

De Grazia, E. Diversion from the Criminal Process: The Mental Health Experiment, Vol. 6, Connecticut Law Review, (1974), pp. 432–528.

Giarretto, H. Humanistic Treatment of Father-Daughter Incest, in *Child Abuse and Neglect: The Family and the Community.*

Helfer, R. & Kempe, C. H. (eds.): Ballinger Publishing Co., 1976.

Johnson, C. Child Sexual Abuse Case Handling Through Public Social Agencies in the Southeast of the USA, *Child Abuse and Neglect: The International Journal,* 5(2), 123–128.

MacFarlane, K. Sexual Abuse of Children. In *The Victimization of Women,* Chapman, J., and Gates, M. (eds.) Beverly Hills: Sage Publishing Co., 1978.

Newman, D., *Convictions: The Determination of Guilt or Innocence Without Trial.* Boston: Little, Brown and Company, 1966.

Nimmer, R. *Diversion: The Search for Alternative Forms of Prosecution.* Chicago: American Bar Foundation, 1974.

Performance Standards and Goals for Pretrial Release and Diversion—Pretrial Diversion, National Association of Pretrial Services Agencies, 1978, Washington, D.C.

Progress Report to the Law Enforcement Assistance Administration, U.S. Department of Justice, May 31, 1979, Sexual Assault Center, Seattle, Washington, D.C.

Rosett, A. & Cressey, D. *Justice by Consent, Plea Bargains in the American Courthouse,* New York: J. B. Lippincott Company, 1976.

Sgroi, S. Introduction: A National Needs Assessment for Protecting Child Victims of Sexual Assault. In *Sexual Assault of Children and Adolescents.,* Burgess, A., Groth, A. N., Holmstrom, L. L., & Sgroi, S.M. (eds). Washington DC: Heath and Company, 1978, xv–xxii.

CLINICAL ISSUES
IN CHILD SEXUAL ABUSE

Lucy Berliner, MSW
Doris Stevens, MA, ACSW

Introduction

It is the authors' observation that the values and generic skills of social work make it an obvious and competent profession to address the societal and individual problems of child sexual abuse. Yet social workers have often overlooked and minimized the extent and effects of this rampant form of child abuse. This chapter will: examine the reluctance of social workers to become involved in treatment and prevention of this problem; describe the extent and dynamics of child sexual abuse; and recommend educational efforts so that social workers in the future are prepared to intervene more effectively on behalf of sexually abused children. These observations and recommendations are based on the authors' seven years of clinical experiences treating sexually abused children of all ages.

Social Workers' Reluctance

Many clinical social workers are in settings where the sexual abuse of children is likely to be discovered, directly or indirectly (e.g., family counseling agencies, medical social work settings, juvenile court systems, child protection agencies). Yet social work, along with other mental health and health care professionals, until very recently, has done a poor job of even acknowledging the problem of child sexual abuse.

There is a strong mythical belief that children tell fantasy stories about being sexually involved with adults. It happens often, in these authors' experience, that when adults first hear a child reporting sexual abuse, they immediately question whether or not the reported event actually occurred. Using too literal an interpretation of Freud's Oedipal stages of development, it has been possible for

93

professionals to rationalize that children often fantasize about reports of coercive sexual activities with adults (Peters, 1976; Herman and Hirshman, 1977). At one point in the study of this subject, Freud himself admitted an error in conceptualization due to the fact he was unable to acknowledge emotionally that the numerous histories of sexual abuse female patients reported to him were actually real (Rush, 1977). Social work practice often reflects a general societal inhibition about the open discussion of sexuality, especially the absence of generally accepted definitions of responsible versus irresponsible sexual behavior. To some, the idea of children being sexual with adults has been too abhorrent to consider. Sometimes, when a situation of ongoing sexual activity between adult and child was uncovered, social workers have been confused about how to respond (i.e., how to judge the appropriateness of the involvement or how to intervene). It may be that personal ambiguous feelings on the part of workers have produced this response, or it may be due to an incomplete understanding of sexuality and the entire range of functional human sexual response, including child sexuality.

The authors have heard many reports from clients which indicate that social workers sometimes have acknowledged the existence of sexual abuse with their clients but have minimized its impact. When women clients have brought up the subject, they have been told to "try to forget it," "it's in the past and you need to concentrate on present relationships." The natural difficulty in talking about sexual abuse is exacerbated by discounting or therapist reluctance. With victims, especially young children, there is an attitude that sexual abuse is not a serious enough mental health problem to justify intervention or that the intervention may cause trauma which outweighs the abuse. Some promote the idea that adult-child sex is acceptable in some sub-groups or results from peculiar cultural or socioeconomic conditions like poverty, overcrowding or rural isolation. If the child demonstrates severe dysfunction then s/he becomes the focus of the intervention process. The worker may even concentrate on what about the child's personality or behavior caused the victimization. The abusive behavior is ignored or is treated as a relatively unimportant symptom of deeper psychological problems in one or more actors in the situation. Treatment plans have addressed marital discord, alcoholism, stress, family conflict, and child behavior problems instead of the sexual abuse, with the assumption that the abuse will disappear if these other problems are cured. All these responses fail to validate the child's experience.

Clinical Definitions

Sexual abuse of children is a major social and clinical problem. Based on retrospective studies, current estimates are that one in five girls and one in eleven boys is sexually molested (Finkelhor, 1979a; Sarafino, 1979). Victimization surveys suggest that one in ten women is raped, most of them young, and many teenagers (*Uniform Crime Reports*, 1977). This means that a significant portion of the child population is involved by adults in activity which is illegal and which is considered an abnormal event in the process of human growth and development. Although there is evidence that adult-child sexual activity has occurred throughout history, it has traditionally been prohibited and has not existed openly as accepted practice (Rush, 1980). Yet, the cultural sanctions have not only failed to control the incidence of child sexual abuse, but have inhibited children from reporting such activity. One study reported that two-thirds of girls and three-fourths of boys had not told of the abuse and it is generally believed that most cases do not come to the attention of the authorities (Finkelhor, 1979a).

Sexual victimization is coercive or nonconsenting sexual activity. Whenever there are sexual acts between adult and child they are always coercive because a child is unable to give truly informed consent to such a relationship (Finkelhor, 1979b). Children are physically and psychologically dependent on adults and thus are not in a position of equality. Children also are unequal to adults in not previously having experienced sexual relationships. In an unequal relationship, true consent is not possible. Adult sexual contact with a child is behavior which the offender (usually male) engages in for his own pleasure without regard for the effects on the child. He does it even though outlets for adult consenting relationships are readily available to him (Groth and Birnbaum, 1979). This sexual activity is not within the range of normal adult sexual behavior or normal childhood experience.

Children are victims of a range of types of sexual abuse. There are many terms for different kinds of sexual victimization which vary between jurisdictions and among professionals. Some examples are: molestation; child sexual abuse; sexual assault; rape; indecent liberties; incest; statutory rape; contributing to the delinquency of a minor for immoral purposes; child pornography; sexual misuse. Most of these are legal terms (in one jurisdiction or another) and some are terms used commonly by the professions and the lay public as well. For purposes of clarification and analysis in this chapter, sexual victimization of children will be categorized into three groupings: rape, child sexual abuse, and sexual exploitation. These definitions, based on the degree of coercion used and the relationship between child and offender, are derived from the authors' clinical experience.

Rape is usually a single violent act accompanied by the use of a weapon, physical force or a threat of harm. The offender may be a stranger, but is more often an acquaintance of the victim. *Child sexual abuse* involves an adult, almost always someone known or related to the child, using his/her position of authority to coerce the child into sexual activity. If the offender continues to have access to the child, it is likely that the abuse will be repeated. *Sexual exploitation* refers to situations in which the child/adolescent considers him/herself old enough to be able to consent to a sexual relationship and does not necessarily perceive him/herself as a victim. However, the adult uses the inequal power relationship between himself and the child/adolescent to exploit that child. This may mean there is a significant age difference between the teen and adult, or the teen might be mentally or emotionally delayed.

Rape

Rape is most commonly associated with adolescents, although some assaults on young children are clearly rape. The sexual acts are usually forced intercourse—oral, vaginal and anal. Injury is not uncommon, resulting either from the act or from the process of securing submission of the victim. Adolescent victims are almost always girls and the offenders are peers or older males. When the victim is a young child, the rape is often brutal and includes abduction.

> Example: Three-year-old N. (male) was taken by a seventeen-year-old neighborhood boy to an isolated spot where he bound the young child's hands and feet and inserted objects into his rectum. The little boy was abused for several hours, in a repetitive manner, and then released to be found wandering.

The circumstances of the assault when the victim is a teenager often involve situations which entail a high amount of risk or an activity from which the teenager has been restricted. Common circumstances include accepting a ride or meeting someone at a party, alcohol and drug involvement or being a runaway. Although it is normal adolescent behavior to test limits and challenge adult authority, this may make them vulnerable to sexual assault, less likely to report, and more likely to be blamed for the victimization.

Example: Fifteen-year-old A. accepted a ride on her way to school. The man asked if she wanted to smoke some "weed." After A. agreed, he took her to a wooded area, pulled a knife and said he would kill her if she didn't do what he said. He forced vaginal and oral penetration of A.

The physical and psychological response to a rape is called "rape trauma syndrome" (Burgess and Holmstrom, 1974). This syndrome refers to a cluster of symptoms commonly seen in victims of rape. It is a traumatic reaction to a sudden, unanticipated violent act which includes physical complaints, sleep and appetite disturbances, inability to concentrate, phobias, fear responses immediately following the act, as well as longer term adjustment reactions and life changes. Adolescents differ from adult rape victims in that they are less likely to seek help with the emotional sequelae and often deny any effects. There is some evidence that teenage victims displace the consequences which may surface later (Burgess, Groth, Holmstrom and Sgroi, 1978).

Sexual Abuse

Child sexual abuse includes a range of sexual acts, including touching the genitals, forced masturbation, digital penetration, oral-genital contact, intracrural intercourse, and vaginal and anal penetration. Other sexual activities which are imposed on children are voyeurism, exposure, and involvement in photography or filming for pornographic purposes.

Child sexual abuse usually involves young children. In one large sample of 730 child sexual assault victims (16 years and younger), who sought services over a one year period, almost two-thirds were under twelve years old at the time of disclosure and 41 per cent were under eight years old (Sexual Assault Center, 1980). Even infants are known to be molested. The victims are both boys and girls with some reported populations ranging up to one-third male victims (Children's Hospital, 1979). The offender is usually an adult male who is known to or related to the child victim. More than half of reported cases involve a family member as the offender, with a parent or parent figure the largest group of offenders at 42 per cent. Other family offenders are usually brothers, grandfathers or uncles. Only 13% of child victims are assaulted by strangers (i.e., rape situations) with the remainder by family friends, neighbors, babysitters or individuals who work with children, such as coaches, youth-leaders, counselors, and teachers. Boys are somewhat more likely to be victimized by nonfamily members and girls by family members (Sexual Assault Center, 1980). In those few cases involving adult female offenders they are usually either involved with a male offender as well, or are psychotic. Among adolescents who sexually abuse young children, there are increasing numbers of female offenders being reported (Wenet, 1981).

Sexual Exploitation

Sexual exploitation involves a continuum of degrees of inequality between partners. In some cases the difference is one of age where an older man or woman prefers younger partners and the issue is that of greater sophistication or life experiences in the older person. In other cases there is a disparity of power as well as age, such as an older person in a position of authority. Where there is an obviously unequal situation such as teacher-student, employer-employee or counselor-client, at any age the possibility of exploitation exists. Even when the teenager actively pursues the relationship s/he is not always equipped to handle it and the adult must be able to handle the situation. The ultimate and most insidious form of exploitation is financial, where children are paid for participation in pornography or prostitution rings for the benefit of adults. These are usually teenagers who have run away or who are alienated from the mainstream already and have few survival choices or skills other than selling their bodies.

Offenders

The offender uses some type of coercion to involve the child in sexual activity. It may be force, threat, pressure, misrepresentation of moral standards, exploitation, or simple exertion of adult authority. Different kinds of coercion may be used at various times or with different victims by the same offender. Most offenders do not commit a sexual act which physically harms the child or use more force than necessary to insure the child's cooperation (Groth, 1976). Only one-third of reported child sexual assault cases involve a single incident of abuse. When the offender is not a family member, multiple incidents occur in about one-third of the cases and when it is a family member, more than 85 per cent of cases involve repeated abuse. It is not uncommon for the abuse to go on for years in family situations (Sexual Assault Center, 1980).

There is no general agreement on what causes an individual to commit a sexual offense. Explanations differ depending on the model for understanding human behavior (e.g., psychodynamic, behavioral, or systems theory). Although the motivation of the offender is not entirely understood, there are some generally agreed upon characteristics of the offender population (Groth and Birnbaum, 1979; Giarretto, 1976; Summit and Kryso, 1978; Burgess et al. 1978; Butler, 1978). Only a few sexual offenders suffer from major mental illness (e.g., schizophrenia, manic depressive illness) or organic syndromes such as senility. A few are mentally retarded, but most are of average intelligence. A small percentage of child offenders are antisocial with generalized criminal backgrounds, and the child abuse is part of a pervasive pattern of abusing others.

The majority of sexual offenders against children are individuals who otherwise seem relatively normal. Although there is a wide range of individual personality styles, the offender is generally functioning adequately in society. Most are employed, support the family and don't have criminal records. In some cases, the man is active in community or church affairs, and highly regarded by others. Child offenders characteristically are self-centered, immature, insecure men who have difficulty with interpersonal relationships. Many of them were physically or sexually abused as children or grew up in a home in which there was abuse toward others. (Groth, 1979) In a significant number of cases, alcoholism is present as a problem as well. Probably, certain personality characteristics (such as shyness, inadequacies, lack of confidence), in combination with childhood experiences (e.g., sexual or physical abuse) and/or situational factors (e.g., loss of job, other stresses) can lead to a pattern of sexual offending against a child. This pattern begins in adolescence for many offenders (Children's Hospital, 1979; Wenet, 1981). Becoming a sexual offender does not occur suddenly. It is a gradual process, beginning with thoughts and fantasies (elaborate mental scenarios about sexual encounters) and finally leading to the actual commission of the act (Abel, 1979; McGuire, 1965). This process often includes repeated masturbation to these deviant fantasies. Since the offender knows it is wrong to molest a child, he rationalizes the behavior by calling it something else (e.g., "sex education"), by blaming external factors ("I was drinking"; "she wanted it"; "my wife turned me down"), or by minimizing the extent or impact ("it was only a few times"; "it didn't hurt her"). This cognitive distortion allows for repetition of the offending behavior, which almost always continues until it is interrupted by some outside force: disclosure, or no available victim.

Sexual offenders have different patterns of offending. An offender may abuse girls or boys, or both. He/she might abuse many different children or one child many times, singly, in pairs, or even groups of children. He/she might prefer children of a particular age or appearance. Some offenders only abuse non-family members, others only their own children, and some both. The sexual abuse may be intermittent, it may be a series of compulsively repetitive acts, or may change over time.

Patterns of Abuse

It is clear that children are exposed to a wide variety of sexual abuse situations. It is determined primarily by the offender and his/her style of victimization. The offender will generally continue to attempt molestation as long as he has access to the child, the child does not talk, or he does not get caught.

> Example: T. & C., seven and eight year old girls, went to the school yard after hours to play; they met a friendly man who said he would show them something. He then pulled out his penis and asked them to touch it. The girls refused and ran home immediately to report the incident to their parents.

The abuse might be an ongoing situation involving one child, who for some reason accepts the sexual contact in exchange for meeting emotional or social needs.

> Example: An eight-year-old girl, S., used to go to the next door neighbor's house often in the afternoons after school. It seemed to her family that S. was very attached to the neighbor

and received much attention, as well as little gifts, from him. Two years later, it came out that the neighbor had made S. suck his penis and masturbate him during these visits.

Or it might be a group situation involving many children. Offenders may establish a "ring" of children who participate in the sexual activities as part of initiation or group membership (Burgess, 1981).

Example: Thirteen-year-old D. and six of his male friends used to go to the offender's house after their paper routes because he would talk to them about sex and show them dirty magazines. Then he would make them perform sexual acts, with him and with each other. This was disclosed three years later.

Although most offenders tend to either abuse outside the family or within, some offenders molest children both in and out of the family.

Example: K's father had molested her since age five. When she turned ten, he began to also force her friends to perform oral sex on him. He would involve them in a sexual game of "truth or consequences" and would pay the girls with cigarettes, jewelry, or money. Eight other girls were eventually identified as victims.

When the abuse occurs within a family, it usually involves the oldest female child. In one-third of intrafamily sexual abuse cases, more than one child is victimized (Conte and Berliner, 1981). There is a range of types of sexual abuse, even within families.

Example: E. is an eighteen-year-old whose mother was schizophrenic. From age eight, E. took over many of the usual responsibilities of wife and mother. She cared for the younger children and did much of the housekeeping. Her father told her many times he would like to marry her. Father began introducing her to sex with him at age eight and demanded intercourse regularly in her teen years.

Example: T. was molested by her alcoholic father from age eight to fifteen. He would come to her bed and fondle her genitals and sometimes masturbate against her body. She pretended she was asleep during the sexual abuse incidents. Her mother knew nothing of the occurrences.

The variety of sexual abuse situations clearly would not produce a uniform response among victims. Although there are general similarities in the dynamics of various forms of sexual abuse, the individual victim's response can best be interpreted by understanding the characteristics of the particular abuse situation.

Disclosure

Most children do not report the sexual abuse directly to authorities. About 15 per cent of reported cases are discovered by someone hearing or seeing something and investigating further (Conte and Berliner, 1981). For example, the child's behavior has changed or s/he exhibits reluctance to be with a certain person. Some very young children may not know sexual abuse is wrong because the offender is a trusted adult; if the acts are not violent, the child would have no source of information about the meaning of the sexual contact. Other children may suspect that no one will believe them. In some cases, the child meets other needs by maintaining the secret and therefore does not want to tell. Most offenders warn or threaten the child to remain silent, and since children do not expect adults to be wrong, these threats can be very effective. Many children, because of developmental limitations, are not able to accurately assess the adults' responsibility for the abusive behavior and believe they will be responsible for the consequences of disclosure. The offender may suggest to the child that whatever happens as a result of telling about the abuse will be the child's fault (e.g., family will break up, someone will go to jail, mother will have a nervous breakdown).

The reasons for disclosure are many. Most children tell a parent, even if there has been a delay since the incident(s). Children may tell because the abuse is escalating or progressing to other children. They might tell because of a situation change which makes the child feel it is now safe to disclose (e.g., mother has decided to divorce the offender), or because s/he is now old enough to assert him/herself. Sometimes it comes out for reasons unrelated to the sexual abuse, such as a parent-child conflict over rules. A significant percent of children tell other people, like a peer who then tells her parents or a school counselor. A history of sexual abuse might also emerge in the context of counseling for other problems.

Effects on Children

The full impact of sexual victimization is not known. The effect on any individual child varies. Some children may exhibit symptoms of distress while it is occurring; others begin to show symptoms at disclosure, and some have a delayed response. Some children do not appear affected, although most have at least a transient situational reaction. A few children are clearly seriously and permanently damaged. Children may have physical consequences, such as venereal disease. There is evidence of an association between runaway, prostitution, drug abuse, sexual dysfunction, and other adjustment problems and a history of sexual abuse (James and Meyerding, 1977; Benward and Densen-Gerber, 1975; McGuire and Wagner, 1978; Tsai, 1978). The relationship between sexual abuse and psychiatric disorders is just beginning to be explored—for example, hysterical seizures (Goodwin, 1979). It is known that a significant number of child sex offenders were themselves sexually abused as children and that many rapists were victims of sexual exploitation during childhood (Groth, 1979). The large numbers of women who were abused as children and are seeking help for the effects in their adult lives is evidence that although a person can function, the consequences may be long-lasting (Tsai and Wagner, 1978). Most children do recover from the observable effects of sexual abuse and grow up to function adequately. But the insidious and often long-term effects on life choices and self-image are extremely difficult to measure.

Almost all victims express a sense of feeling guilty or responsible to some extent for the abuse or its aftermath. Few children forget about what happened and report feeling that something about them is bad, ugly, or damaged because of the abuse. In terms of the immediate impact on a child, the abuse can be viewed as an abnormal event interrupting the normal developmental process. Like other experiences in a child's life, many factors influence the ability of a particular child to successfully integrate the experience and cope with the effects. There are certain issues which are important in understanding the process of recovery. For example, factors concerning the sexual abuse events themselves may be related to adjustment. When violence is used or threatened or the child is injured, it almost always produces a fear response. The child behaves fearfully, has nightmares, clings to the parent and exhibits regressed behavior. Children who are physically threatened or abused over time may become withdrawn, sullen, or defiant.

The significance the relationship between child and offender has on the impact of sexual abuse is related to the extent to which the child depends on the offender to meet physical or psychological needs. When there are other positive or neutral aspects of the relationship the child may want the abuse, but not the relationship, to end. When the offender is a parent, there is always a major impact because the parent-child relationship is clearly defined with the expectation of meeting needs for protection, nurturance, and love. If a parent sexually abuses his/her child, the basic trust is permanently impaired, and can never be completely restored. The child may learn that acceptance or love is related to the exchange of sexual favors, and this can significantly influence future relationships.

Who the offender is also influences others' responses to the child's report at disclosure. Adults find it hard to accept that a person they like, respect or depend on would sexually abuse a child and, accordingly, might prefer to believe the child is lying. When believing the child's report requires some change or action on the part of the parent, it may be easier to discount. The child who is believed and supported will have the best chance for recovery. For the child who does not tell at all, or waits many years to tell, the impact of not telling also influences recovery.

The child's developmental stage at the time of abuse may significantly affect the impact of the abuse. The child might be too young to even remember, or understand the meaning of the behavior. An older child could understand, but not be able to integrate an experience which is premature and foreign to her/his own age level and peers' experiences. S/he may expend much energy, for example, keeping the knowledge of the sexual abuse and her "differentness" hidden from others. If the abuse occurs over time, the child may be prevented from having the normal childhood experiences which form the basis for healthy adult adjustment. This lack of synchronization between level of maturity and life experiences is disruptive and alienating. There may also be coincidental situational events, such as a death in the family or a divorce, which compound the reaction to the abuse. The family may have other problems, such as physical violence, mental illness, developmental or physical disability, alcoholism, financial or marital problems.

The individual child's personality figures in the coping style and the consequences of the abuse. Children are different and have clearly established personalities at a young age. Shy children or late developing adolescents might be targets for victimization, simply because they already feel different. Individual children handle similar sexual abuse situations in different ways; one child might deny and dissociate the experience, another might be defiant and fight back, while another would accommodate and participate. Finally, the process of intervention is also likely to affect the subsequent adjustment of the child. Following disclosure, the child must be protected from further victimization, both physical and psychological, to enhance recovery. Until the offender is separated from the child and receives treatment, there is a strong possibility that re-offenses will occur. Even when the child is not being sexually abused, there is a good possibility, following disclosure, that offender and/or other family members will blame, tease, or further harass the child. The protection of the child may be accomplished by the family without official intervention, or may require the involvement of the child protection and legal authorities. There are many possible outcomes and changes in the child's life following disclosure, such as out-of-home placement, divorce, or moving. Since intervention is always disruptive to some extent, it is important that the personnel and the processes be devoted to providing support to the child and minimizing further trauma. When the offender admits the abuse and cooperates with intervention, the protective services and criminal justice system involvement is minimal and generally not traumatic.

The impact of sexual abuse on a child depends on a variety of factors, including the sexual abuse characteristics, personality and developmental stage of the child, the child's family and support system, and what transpires as a result of telling. Treatment planning should be geared to the specific needs of the child victim, with the goals of restoring the child to normal functioning and alleviating the negative effects of the sexual victimization.

Education for Social Workers

Social work is a particularly appropriate profession for addressing the complex social and clinical problem of child sexual assault, because it has as its basic approach understanding individual behavior in the context of all related social systems. However, to fulfill this responsibility change in social work education is necessary. For this particular social problem, the sexually offensive behavior must be understood as more than individual psychopathology. It is coercive and criminal conduct imposed on other persons, and therefore successful outcome requires the involvement of social and legal systems as well as clinical intervention. Clinical intervention to assist a child victim's recovery can only be effective in a safe and supportive environment. An advocate approach for the child can insure that system-induced trauma is minimized so that intervention with the victim on an individual basis is optimal. For offenders, their reluctance to seek treatment is well known; court supervision can insure their participation. The social worker must learn to understand the related legal and social systems so that the offender receives effective treatment and so that society is protected.

Social workers can work to identify and change institutional responses which have supported the continued victimization of children—for example, insensitive medical and legal personnel who through their style of interviewing have placed blame and guilt on the child victim. To empower the weaker and disenfranchised members of society is consistent with social work history and values. The tools of community education and organization, training and consultation can be used to improve the health care, mental health, criminal justice and children's protective service systems' responses for all children. Social workers need to be provided knowledge about child sexual assault and systems involved, and also to be sensitized to the problem. Specific protocols for addressing various aspects of the problem (e.g., interviewing, medical care, and legal procedures for sexually abused children) should be taught.

In order for social workers to be effective in helping sexually abused children, a willingness to act vigorously on behalf of the victim is necessary. Social work needs to confront the barriers to learning about this serious mental health and social problem; this could be done in conjunction with the study of other types of violence against persons. Courses addressing spouse battering, abuse of the elderly, rape and general child abuse as well as child sexual abuse, need to be added to the basic social work curriculum.

Social workers also need to examine their personal values about child sexual abuse. This can perhaps best be done in a course of study on human sexuality. It is not possible to understand child sexual abuse without the backdrop of a full understanding of the range of functional human sexual response and associated values. The value of consent as a critical component of sexual relationships is a point for education and values clarification.

A strong link between curriculum and the practicing field is important for educating social workers on child sexual abuse. There has been a proliferation of service programs in recent years, which have not yet researched and published their findings on intervention in child sex abuse but nevertheless have valuable experiences to share. Exposure to the legal, medical, and child protection system is essential. Practicum placements in agencies serving sexually abused children, coupled with the classroom experiences suggested above, would provide the best preparation. There is a tremendous need for research on child sexual abuse. Survey data on the extent of the problem in our society is minimal. Longitudinal studies to document effects or to measure impacts of intervention have not yet been successfully conducted. Social work researchers can make a significant contribution by addressing a variety of questions on child sexual abuse in a manageable research design. Questions about immediate and long-term impacts, how adjustment varies among children, offender treatment models, the relationship between sexual abuse and psychiatric problems, and prevention are all areas that desperately need to be informed by empirical data.

Conclusion

Child sexual abuse is still not fully understood. The magnitude of the problem in contrast to the stated social value against such activity cannot be ignored. Currently, social and political values reflected in the major institutions of society fail to successfully control this behavior and may in fact reinforce sexual (and other types of) exploitation of children. Social work needs to educate itself to learn the facts about sexual abuse of children and the results on our population so the profession can take more responsibility for: creating awareness of the problem; uncovering it; distinguishing between functional, affectionate activity and abusive behavior; stopping abusive behavior; offering hope in the form of concrete services for change; advocating for the child (and family) in other systems; and preventing future abuse.

REFERENCES

Abel, G. G., Becker, J. V., Murphy, W. D., and Flanagan, B. *Identifying dangerous child molesters*. Presented at the Eleventh Banff International Conference on Behavior Modification 1979.
Benward, J., and Densen-Gerber, J. Incest as a causative factor in antisocial behavior: An exploratory study. *Contemporary Drug Problems*, 1975, 4(3), 323–340.
Burgess, A. W., Groth, A., Holmstron, L. L., and Sgroi, S.M. *Sexual assault of children and adolescents*. Lexington, Mass.: Lexington Books, 1978.

Burgess, A.W., Groth, A. N., McCausland, M.P. Child sex initiation rings. *American Journal of Orthopsychiatry*, 1981, 51(1), 110–119.

Burgess, A. W., and Holstrom, L.L. Rape trauma syndrome. *American Journal of Psychiatry*, 1974, 131(9), 981–986.

Butler, S. *Conspiracy of Silence: The Trauma of Incest.* San Francisco: New Glide Publications, 1978.

Children's Hospital National Medical Center, Child Protection Center-Special Unit, Washington, D.C. Personal communication, 1979.

Conte, J.R., and Berliner, L. Sexual abuse of children: Implications for practice. *Social Casework*, 1981, 62(10), 601–606.

Finkelhor, D. *Sexually victimized children.* New York: Free Press, 1979.

Finkelhor, D. What's wrong with sex between adults and children? Ethics and the problem of sexual abuse. *American Journal of Orthopsychiatry*, 1979, 49(4), 692-296.

Giarretto, H. Humanistic treatment of father-daughter incest. In R. E. Helfer and C. H. Kempe (Eds), *Child abuse and neglect—the family and community.* Michigan State University: Ballenger Publications, 1976.

Goodwin, J. Hysterical seizures: A sequel to incest. *American Journal of Orthopsychiatry*, 1979, 49(4), 698–703.

Groth, A. N. *Child sexual assault: Dominance, authority and aggression.* Paper presented at the American Association of Psychiatric Services for Children, 28th Annual Meeting, San Francisco 1976.

Groth, A. N. Sexual trauma in the life histories of rapists and child molesters. *Victimology: An International Journal*, 1979, 4(1), 10–16.

Groth, A. N. and Birnbaum, H. J. Adult sexual orientation and attraction to under-age persons. *Archives of Sexual Behavior*, 1978, 7(3), 175–181.

Groth, A. N. and Birnbaum, H. J. *Men who rape: The psychology of the offender.* New York: Plenum Press, 1979.

Herman, J. and Hirschman, L. Father-daughter incest. *Signs: Journal of Women in Culture and Society*, 1977, 2(4), 735–756.

James, J. and Meyerding, J. Early sexual experience as a factor in prostitution. *Archives of Sexual Behavior*, 1977, 7(1), 31–42.

McGuire, R. L., Carlisle, J. N., and Young, B. G. Sexual deviations as conditioned behavior: A hypothesis. *Behavior Research and Therapy*, 1965, 2, 185–190.

McGuire, L.S., and Wagner, N. Sexual dysfunction in women who were molested as children: One response pattern and suggestions for treatment. *Journal of Sex and Marital Therapy*, 1978, 4(1), 11–15.

Peters, J.J. Children who are victims of sexual assault and the psychology of offenders. *American Journal of Psychotherapy*, 1976, 3(3), 398–421.

Rush, R. *The best kept secret: Sexual abuse of children.* Englewood Cliffs, New Jersey: Prentice-Hall, 1980.

Rush, F. The Freudian cover-up. *Chrysallis*, 1977, 31–45.

Sarafino, E.P. An estimate of nationwide incidence of sexual offenses against children. *Child Welfare*, 1979, 58(2), 127–134.

Sexual Assault Center, Harborview Medical Center. *Client characteristics—1980.* Seattle, Washington, 1980.

Summit, R. and Kryso, J. Sexual abuse of children: A clinical spectrum. *American Journal of Orthopsychiatry*, 1978, 48(2), 237–251.

Tsai, M. and Wagner, N. Therapy groups for women sexually molested as children. *Archives of Sexual Behavior*, 1978, 7(5), 417–427.

Uniform Crime Reports for the United States. Washington, D.C.: F.B.I., 1977.

Wenet, G. Juvenile Sex Offender Program, Adolescent Clinic, University of Washington. Peronal communication, 1981.

FAMILY TREATMENT
OF CHILD SEXUAL ABUSE*

Suzanne M. Sgroi, MD

Family Treatment means family therapy to many helping services professionals. They further assume that family therapy is the treatment of choice for incest cases, that it should begin immediately whenever possible, and that family treatment is not indicated for other types of child sexual abuse. These are all misconceptions. Some degree of family treatment is nearly always indicated in both intrafamily and extrafamily cases. Instead of limiting therapeutic intervention to family therapy, a variety of treatment modalities should be employed with families of children who have been sexually victimized. When family therapy *is* utilized, it should be employed in conjunction with other treatment modalities and should not begin until individual therapeutic relationships have been established with key family members.

This chapter first addresses the type and degree of family treatment required by the various types of child sexual abuse cases. Then the treatment needs of the incestuous family and various family treatment modalities are described. The concluding sections of this chapter discuss development of family treatment programs and treatment outcomes. Readers are referred to *A Handbook of Clinical Intervention in Child Sexual Abuse* (Sgroi, 1982) for a detailed description of working with involuntary clients and the psychosocial equivalent of total life support— both key concepts in family treatment of child sexual abuse.

My suggested approach to family treatment is based on observations and experience drawn from approximately 600 cases of child sexual abuse for which I have provided direct services or consulta-

---

*This chapter is based on a more extensive chapter in Sgroi, Suzanne M., *A Handbook of Clinical Intervention in Child Sexual Abuse*, Lexington, Massachusetts: Lexington Books, 1982.

tion since 1972. These cases presented in various settings: the hospital emergency room, a walk-in venereal disease clinic, and a pilot child sexual abuse treatment program operated by the Connecticut Department of Children and Youth Services from 1977–1979** In addition to serving as program developer for the above family treatment project, I have frequently been asked to evaluate cases of child sexual abuse and to provide consultation to the police and child protective services staff. Despite the multiple referral sources, there have been far more similarities in presenting characteristics, ongoing dynamics and responses to intervention than differences in these cases. Nevertheless, in view of the recent rapid expansion and development of knowledge about child sexual abuse, I would advise other helping services professionals to test the following approach and recommendations for family treatment in the light of their own case experience.

Indications for Family Treatment

Assessment of Family Contribution

A family assessment should be conducted in every validated case of child sexual abuse regardless of the identity of the perpetrator. Although a lengthy assessment process may not be necessary, the strengths and weaknesses of *every* family member should be identified as they may contribute to intervention outcomes. The family's *contribution* to the sexual abuse must also be assessed. Was the child's victimization a capricious event with an unknown outside perpetrator whose access to the child was accidental, totally unforeseeable and completely beyond the control of the parents or guardians? Although incidents of this type *do* occur, they are exceedingly rare. Instead, most cases of child sexual abuse involve perpetrators who are known to the child and interactions which are, in large measure, predictable and preventable. Assessing the type and degree of family contribution to the child's sexual victimization is key to determining indications for family treatment. The following issues should be examined for all cases.

**Supported in part by a grant from the National Center for Child Abuse and Neglect. Department of Health and Human Services (NCCAN 90-C-399).

1. Poor supervision. Often children are sexually abused because of poor supervition by their parents or caretakers. In other words, the child is placed at risk for sexual abuse through the omission of a responsible adult. For example, a child who lives in a home where adults are frequently engaging in sexual activity with multiple caretakers is at great risk for sexual abuse, even if the caretaker has no intention of involving the child. The youngster's exposure to many adults who are engaging in casual sexual encounters with his or her parent or guardian is confusing at best, but may be downright dangerous since transient sexual partners are less likely to observe usual societal limits.

An example of poor supervision outside the home involves parents who permit young children to frequent public places such as restaurants or bars, especially at late hours and unaccompanied by a responsive caretaker. Parents who do not screen and set limits on their children's playtimes, playmates and play areas are also exercising poor supervision. This is not to say that parents or guardians can or should exercise direct oversight of their school-age children on a 24 hour basis. However, many cases of child sexual abuse are occurring within a milieu of complete parental abdication of supervisory responsibility. Such children are likely to be perceived by their parents as "able to take care of themselves," even at ages five or six years.

Whenever poor supervision inside or outside the home has contributed to the sexual abuse of a child, parental assumption of appropriate supervisory responsibility becomes a family treatment issue. The odds are that a pattern of lack of parental supervision will be present rather than an isolated lapse. It is also likely that changing the pattern will require more than simply calling attention to the problem. Role modeling by the therapist and peer group reinforcement after discussion and demonstration of appropriate parental supervision will usually be required for significant change to take place. If it does not, the child may be sexually abused again.

2. Poor choice of surrogate caretakers or babysitters. Children are often sexually abused by surrogate caretakers or babysitters. Again, it is the responsibility of parents and guardians to select individuals who will be responsible for their children with great care. Complaints of sexual abuse of a child by mother's boyfriend who is left to care for the youngster while mother goes shopping or to work occur too frequently to be ignored. Adolescents are often used as babysitters for children with no thought given to the fact that adolescence is a stage of intense sexual curiosity and exploration. If appropriate limits are not set and enforced, adolescent babysitters often invite their friends to "keep them company" while they are ostensibly taking care of children. Sometimes a friend will instigate the sexual abuse of the child unbeknownst to the babysitter. Other times, the babysitter and friend(s) will jointly engage in sexual abuse of their charges. Of course, a related or unrelated babysitter may also sexually abuse a child by himself or herself. Adolescent males are generally inappropriate persons to be chosen as babysitters because, in addition to all the tendency toward sexual exploration associated with that developmental stage, society places fewer inhibitions on aggressive behavior in males than in females.

Child sexual abuse by a surrogate caretaker or babysitter also becomes a family treatment issue. The parent or guardian must accept responsibility for entrusting the child to this person and/or for not setting appropriate limits about visitors to the caretaker or babysitter. If the caretaker or babysitter is a family member or occupies a parental or familial role for the child (e.g., sibling or mother's boyfriend), this issue is further complicated by all the dynamics of intrafamily child sexual abuse.

3. Inappropriate sleeping arrangements. Sometimes the choice of sleeping arrangements for family members will be a contributing factor in child sexual abuse. The practice of "doubling up" children of the opposite sex to sleep together in the same bed or even in the same room also creates an unnecessary risk of inappropriate sexual activity. When there is a significant age disparity between them, sexual abuse of a younger child by an older sibling or cousin may also occur. As Laury (1978) points out, this practice is not limited to lower class families who sleep under crowded conditions because of poverty. Middle class parents may consolidate family sleeping arrangements in order to free a bedroom for use as a family room or den. Whatever the reason, when children of the opposite sex who are agemates regularly sleep together, a level of intimacy is fostered which places them at higher risk for sexual activity with each other. When a younger child sleeps with an adolescent sibling of the opposite sex, he or she is placed at risk for forced or pressured sexual victimization by the adolescent.

Inappropriate sleeping arrangements are an obvious treatment issue which may be difficult to resolve because of associated dynamics. In all probability, the parents' choice to permit inappropriate sleeping arrangements is associated with blurring of role boundaries within the family (see item 4 below).

4. *Blurred role boundaries.* Family interaction characterized by blurring of role boundaries can be both a predisposing factor for as well as a result of intrafamily child sexual aubse. It is mentioned in this section because it is clearly a treatment issue for the family as a whole as well as for individual family members including the victim and the offender. Significant blurring of familial role boundaries can only take place when parents permit this to happen and fail to set appropriate expectations and limits for themselves as well as for the children. Inappropriate genital exposure, lack of privacy with respect to bathroom and sleeping arrangments, and permitting physically intimate behavior by parents and children to occur with children both as witnesses and participants—all are examples of blurring of familial role boundaries which may predispose to child sexual abuse.

Since parents or persons who occupy family power positions are in the best position to clarify role boundaries, this treatment issue must be addressed to insure the future safety of the child. If treatment for this issue is limited to the victim and he or she must continue to live at home, the risk for reoccurrence of the sexual abuse is very great.

5. *Sexual abuse by a family member.* This is an obvious family contribution to child sexual abuse as regards the actions of the perpetrator who is a family member. However, sexual abuse of a child by a single family member usually involves some degree of direct or indirect participation by other family members as well. For example, one family member may "set up" a child to be victimized by another family member. However, incest is more often a result of indirect contribution by every family member. As Poznanski and Blos (1975) point out, in cases of father-daughter incest, the mother has nearly always failed to set or enforce appropriate limites on the interactions between her husband and daughter which preceded the sexual activity.

Unless effective family treatment is provided for cases of intrafamily child sexual abuse, it can be predicted that every family member (father, mother, child victim(s) and siblings) is at risk to act out subsequent scenarios of sexual abuse. This could take the form of repeated sexual abuse of the original victim or sexual abuse of a sibling. If the parents separate, the offending parent may victimize another child (his or her own child or a step-child) if an affiliation with another family takes place. If the non-offending spouse re-marries, there is great risk that he or she will select a partner who will sexually victimize *their* child(ren). Lastly, the child victim and/or siblings may themselves grow up to become sexual offenders. (This is also a possible outcome for child victims of sexual abuse by an outside perpetrator.)

Family Treatment Issues by Category of Sexual Abuse

1. Extrafamily perpetrators. In this category of sexual abuse, perpetrators are likely to be known to the child and his or her family. Almost invariably, the victim's parent or guardian will have permitted the perpetrator to have access to the child as a visitor in the home or else will have entrusted the child's care to the perpetrator. Babysitters, friends of the family, neighbors, daycare or school personnel or adults who work with children in groups are all included in this category. Whenever the child's parent exercised a degree of choice over the perpetrator's access to the child, the following may apply.

Family contribution. In cases involving an outside perpetrator, the family contribution is usually limited to poor supervision or the inappropriate choice of a surrogate caretaker or babysitter. The critical issue is *failure to protect.* Treatment of either variety of family contribution is usually best achieved by some combination of authoritative guidance and peer-group enforcement. A comprehensive community child sexual abuse treatment program could provide a treatment modality that would be helpful (i.e., a functioning parent group for parents to attend for a limited number of sessions in which issues of appropriate supervision and selection of babysitters would be discussed). An important exception should be noted here: sexual abuse by an unrelated surrogate caretaker who nevertheless occupies an important familial role for the child or a spousal relationship for a single parent (e.g. mother's boyfriend). Family treatment issues for the latter are similar to those for child sexual abuse by a family member.

Impact upon the victim. This becomes a family treatment issue because of the perception of family members that a child who has been prematurely introduced to sexuality is somehow magically changed by his or her sexual experience (Burgess and Holmstrom,

1979). The family's perception nearly always reinforces the victim's belief that he or she has been damaged. At minimum, there should be counseling of the child's parents which addresses all of the impact issues for the child as well as the associated treatment implications. In some families, short-term treatment (beyond counseling) will be required to resolve these issues. Siblings will also require counseling and at least one session involving the entire family is indicated to set the tone for the future, to clear the air, and to bring any fears or concerns about the victim into the open. Some degree of family treatment is thus essential to the success of the treatment plan for the victim even in cases of extrafamily child sexual abuse.

2. *Intrafamily (non-parent perpetrator).* This category of child sexual abuse may involve older siblings, cousins, aunts, uncles or members of the extended family as perpetrators. When a child has been sexually abused by a relative who is not a parent and who does not occupy a parental role with respect to the victim the same types of treatment issues apply as with an extra-family perpetrator, but in an expanded form.

Family contribution. This may range from a major contribution to the occurrence of the sexual abuse to none at all. Poor supervision or poor choice of surrogate caretakers may underlie child sexual abuse by a relative who is not a parent. Sometimes an older sibling or cousin or aunt or uncle or some other member of the extended family may be permitted access to the target child with poor supervision or no supervision exercised. The large family picnic or other type of extended family gathering when there may be several hours of unsupervised activity for children ranging from older pre-school age straight through adolescence is a good illustration. Such gatherings may provide an opportunity for older children to pressure or force younger relatives to engage in a variety of sexual activities (including all types of sexual penetration) that go far beyond "acceptable" levels of sexual exploration by age mates. Although the parents or guardians of both the aggressors and the victims may be unaware of the character of the unsupervised activity, their lack of oversight and failure to anticipate the need for supervision become family treatment issues.

Likewise, child sexual abuse may occur when a relative who is not a parent is chosen to be a surrogate caretaker or babysitter. All of the same dynamics pertain as when the poor choice of surrogate caretaker is *not* a family member but with the additional problem of divided loyalty. As Burgess and Holmstrom (1977) aptly described, every family member must make a decision to ally himself or herself with either the perpetrator or victim whenever a child is sexually abused by a relative. Thus the divided loyalty itself becomes another treatment issue as well as the guilt experienced by each family member who must make such a difficult decision, regardless of his or her choice. For the parent or guardian who is responsible for the poor choice of surrogate caretaker, accepting responsibility and dealing with his or her guilt for *that* choice also become treatment issues. Lastly, avoiding future "mistakes" regarding appropriate supervision and choice of surrogate caretakers must be addressed.

Predictably, when the person who has sexually abused the child is a relative, the underlying dynamics will be complex. Therapists should be alerted to look for other types of family contribution to child sexual abuse: i.e., inappropriate sleeping arrangements and blurred role boundaries. Again, it should be noted that these are unlikely to be associated accidentally with child sexual abuse by a family member (the reverse is more likely to be true).

Thus the critical issues regarding family contribution to this category of child sexual abuse are *failure to protect* (as in extrafamily cases) and *failure to set appropriate limits* (re sleeping arrangements and role boundaries). Treatment should again be focused upon the parents since both of the above are clearly parental responsibilities and prerogatives. As before, a combination of authoritative guidance and peer-group reinforcement will probably be most effective. Therapists should anticipate that pressure will be required to engage these parents into an effective treatment program and that a longer period of participation in treatment will be required.

Impact upon the child. In addition to societal and cultural barriers to recognizing the actual impact of child sexual abuse by an extrafamily perpetrator upon a victim, there is an added dimension of "blaming the victim" when the perpetrator is a relative. Therapists must anticipate that divided loyalty (child versus perpetrator) will further complicate this issue. If a stranger or a person who is not a relative is the perpetrator, family members are probably less likely to blame the victim for instigating or failing to halt the sexual activity. However, the degree of blame placed upon the perpetrator and the victim when both are relatives may well be determined by the esteem in which they are held and by their relative value as perceived by other family members. Needless to say, this becomes a major treatment issue when the victim remains within the family after the sexual abuse has been disclosed. If powerful family members decide to hold the victim responsible for the sexually abusive behavior and cannot be swayed in this decision during early intervention, the prognosis for family treatment is poor.

Family response to treatment of the child. Adequate treatment for the victim of child sexual abuse can never take place in a familial vacuum: even when the victim is separated from the rest of the family, their response to his or her treatment is profoundly important. If the treatment is effective, the child's behavior can be expected to change in a variety of ways which will inevitably affect the rest of the family. For example, a child who is fearful, withdrawn and docile may become more assertive and demanding as he or she improves. Although these may be healthy behavior patterns, the child's changed behavior may be perceived as disruptive and unwelcome unless the family's response is anticipated and modified. The parents should be made aware of the impact of the sexual abuse upon the child and the treatment needs which will be addressed in therapy. They should be made a part of the treatment plan as much as possible and be helped to recognize and discourage inappropriate behavior and to reinforce healthy behavior as the child's treatment progresses. They should also be helped to see how their own behavior, especially with respect to blurring of role boundaries and inappropriate expectations of the child, has contributed to the sexual abuse. Unless the latter are modified, the family's response to the child's treatment is likely to be undermining and pehaps even destructive.

3. *Intrafamily (parent or parent-figure perpetrator).* First, all of the treatment issues described for intrafamily child sexual abuse by a non-parent perpetrator may also apply to this category. Perpetrators may be fathers or mothers of the child victim, stepparents, grandparents, or the boyfriend or girlfriend of the child's parent. Fathers and mothers of the child victim obviously belong in this category. Stepparents are included, despite the lack of biological relationship, for the same reason as the boyfriend or girlfriend of the child's parent: i.e., they all occupy a familial role for the child. Grandparents are included in this category of perpetrators because they may also occupy a parental role for the victim. Cases of child sexual abuse by a grandparent may be especially complicated since this individual may also have sexually abused the child's parent in the past.

Family contribution. Three critical issues pertain when a child is sexually abused by a parent or parent figure. They are *failure to protect, failure to set limits,* and *abuse of power.*

Failure to protect obviously applies when poor supervision and poor choice of surrogate caretaker are involved (i.e., when the perpetrator is a non-related boyfriend or girlfriend of the victim's parent). However, this critical issue applies to sexual abuse of a child by a parent, step-parent or grandparent as well. Almost invariably, the non-offending parent(s) failed to protect the child victim in a variety of ways and these will be important treatment issues.

Failure to set limits is always a critical issue in this category of child sexual abuse. The perpetrator clearly failed to set limits on himself or herself; otherwise he or she would not have sexually abused the child. However, all parent figures failed to set limits with respect to blurring of role boundaries and role confusion as an additional family contribution.

Abuse of power is always a critical issue in family treatment of child sexual abuse by a parent or parent-figure. Treatment of the victim must always address this issue, regardless of the identity of the perpetrator or the category of sexual abuse which pertains. However, *abuse of power* tends to be a way of life and a dominant aspect of family interaction in incestuous families. It is emphasized here because it will invariably be the key to family treatment. No significant family treatment will be permitted to take place unless this critical issue is addressed since powerful family members will either block participation by all or else will sabotage therapy for those who do participate.

No child victim of sexual abuse by a parent or parent figure who remains at home with the perpetrator will be safe unless there is family treatment which effectively addresses these three critical issues. It is unlikely that effective family treatment can or will occur in the absence of an authoritative incentive (i.e., the legal justice system). Some combination of individual, group, dyad and family therapy will be required. Treatment efforts must be intensive and long-term for significant improvement to take place.

Impact upon the child. All of the family treatment issues described when the perpetrator is a family member who is not a parent pertain to this category as well. Therapists must anticipate that the victim's parent(s) will be less likely to acknowledge the impact of the sexual abuse upon the child and his or her need for treatment. Conflicts around divided loyalty will be very intense and the parents may choose to support each other and ignore the child's needs rather than make the significant changes in their own behavior that would otherwise be required. They may choose to blame the victim entirely both for the sexual activity and the disruption following disclosure. The parent(s) may also choose to reject the victim and to encourage his or her separation from the family. When this occurs, the child must be separated for his or her own safety and there is little chance that family treatment offers any change for the child to be reunited with the family. On the other hand, the parent(s) may choose to keep the child at home and further abuse power by exerting enormous pressure upon him or her to recant the allegation of sexual abuse and/or stop cooperating with outside authority figures. Again, when this occurs, the prognosis for family treatment is grave.

The minimum acceptable goal for family treatment with respect to impact upon the child is to "build in" at least one functioning adult ally for the child in the home. This person should be the non-offending parent but could also be an older sibling, a grandparent or other family member. If there is no person within the family circle who can serve as a functioning adult ally for the child, the therapist must reluctantly opt for the child to be removed from the home.

Lastly, therapists should be aware that divided loyalty conflicts when the perpetrator is the child's grandparent may be especially problemmatic. The child's parent who is also the child of the offending grandparent has the additional burden of coping with a parental role occupied by the perpetrator. Therapists should anticipate that blaming the victim and rejecting the victim are at least as likely and perhaps even more likely to occur.

Family response to treatment of the child. The family's response as the child victim progresses in treatment will probably be the most important determinant for success or failure. Strong family resistance or hostility can sabotage treatment efforts aimed at the sexually abused child. For example, a youngster who formerly was docile and passive and who performed age-inappropriate tasks without resistance may become much more assertive and unwilling to discharge inappropriate homemaking and/or child care responsibilities. Although these changes may be healthy for the child victim, other family members are likely to react with alarm, hostility, and efforts to restore the status quo. Without some type of family treatment, it is unlikely that the child victim who continues to live at home can ever be "re-programmed" to behave in an age-appropriate fashion or to occupy the role of a child appropriately. If blurred role boundaries were a prominent underlying factor, it is virtually impossible to restructure one without restructuring all. Even youngsters who live away from their families after disclosure of sexual abuse usually see or visit with family members thereafter. It is amazing how quickly a negative family response to the victim's new behaviors (even during a short visit) can undermine gains made over months of treatment. Accordingly, treating the child who has been sexually abused by a parent or a parent figure without family treatment will have limited success whenever the child continues to live at home with the perpetrator who still occupies a power position.

Characteristics and Treatment Needs of Parental Incest Families

Although the underlying premise of this chapter is that some level of family treatment is indicated for all categories of child sexual abuse, it is undeniable that the treatment needs of the incestuous family with a parent or parent figure who is the perpetrator are many and complex. Parental incest families have been appropriately described as character-disordered by Anderson and Shafer (1979) because they are comprised of individuals who exhibit many of the personality characteristics of character-disordered persons. They suggest that a treatment model for the character disordered family should parallel the treatment model for an individual who is character-disordered.

Beavers' (1976) description of pathological families is highly applicable to families in which parental incest has taken place: isolated, closed, energy-draining systems with "little vital interaction with the outside world" and possessing limited adaptive mechanisms or capacity for interval change or growth of individual members. He further describes the most seriously disturbed families as "chaotic, clinging in a sticky lump (the amorphous family ego mass)" and that "dreams, fantasies, and a studied unawareness function in place of goal-directed, active negotiation among persons" (p. 49). For less seriously disturbed or "mid-range" families, Beavers uses the analogy of a "primitive sea animal with one large muscle attached to a jaw" to illustrate their rigidity, limited coping mechanisms and vulnerability. Therapists who have worked with numerous parental incest families are likely to recognize the applicability of Beavers' descriptions. The majority of parental-incest families fall within the "mid-range" category; a smaller but highly memorable proportion are "chaotic" in type.

Assessing the degree and type of family pathology is certainly appropriate for those who would venture to treat parental incest families. The prognosis for treatment of "chaotic" families is extremely poor. The prognosis for treatment of "mid-range" families is more optimistic but should still retain the degree of caution usually employed when forecasting treatment outcomes for individuals who can be described as "character disordered." A careful assessment of family functioning and treatment needs should precede the decisions of whether to treat (or not to treat), who to treat and how to treat. Invariably, the treatment issues described below will pertain for the parent who is the perpetrator of incestuous child sexual abuse; frequently they pertain to the family as a functioning unit and to the other family members as well. Since, by definition, child sexual abuse is perpetrated by someone who occupies a power position over the victim, it is not surprising that the perpetrator usually sets or exemplifies the overall style for the pathological family interaction as well. The characteristics of these cases involved:

Abuse of power. In parental incest families more powerful individuals abuse their positions of power in order to gratify their own needs without regard for the harm to others which may result. This is, of course, exemplified by the parent's choice to engage his or her child in sexual activity in order to gratify non-sexual needs. Groth and Burgess (1977) have demonstrated that most perpetrators are gratifying needs for feeling powerful or in control when they are sexually abusing a child. Child sexual abuse is always an aggressive act by the perpetrator, even when there is no force or violence employed. Aggressive rather than benevolent use of power by the strong against the weak becomes the modus operandi for all family interaction in parental incest families. Since perpetrator and other powerful family members can be expected to continue to abuse power until they are checked, this characteristic becomes the primary family treatment need. Until abuse of power is addressed effectively, there can be little attention to other family characteristics or treatment needs of individual family members.

Fear of authority. Members of parental incest families fear authority for the obvious reason: Authority figures are seen as hostile and threatening because exploitative, rather than benevolent, use of power is practiced and experienced within the family; hence the fear that authority (and power) wielded by others will be destructive to one's self. Beavers (1976) commented:

A strong determinant of family system capability is the assumption of members as to the probable nature of human encounter. Disturbed families behave as if encounters will be oppositional; competent families behave as if encounters will be affiliative. Indeed, it is the author's view that a clinical estimate of this underlying assumption will be of assistance in determining the degree of disturbance in family systems and individuals, without regard for diagnostic type or labels (p. 51).

There tends also to be a guilty flavor to the fear of authority experienced by members of parental incest families—possibly in anticipation of discovery of the incest secret and fear of the consequences of its disclosure.

Fear of authority is largely dealt with by avoidance. When encounters with authority are unavoidable, the member of a parental incest family (although assuming that the interaction will be oppositional) may exhibit a range of behavior from passive to aggressive. Anxiety, suspicion, evasiveness, denial and hostility may all characterize behavior stemming from this family treatment need when a confrontation with authority is anticipated or actually does occur.

Isolation. The parental incest family tends to be isolated and withdrawn from society as a whole. Kempe (1977) has described physically abusive parents as "without lifelines." This description is especially apt for parental incest families, even when a large extended family is available to the nuclear family unit. Fear of authority is an important reason for the isolation; it is easy to perceive the entire outside world as hostile and to cope by avoiding interaction with "outsiders" as much as possible. Powerful family members discourage weaker members from establishing alliances with persons who are outside the nuclear family. The children's friendships and opportunities for socialization away from home are strictly limited or forbidden entirely. Parents, especially incestuous fathers, may establish themselves as the sole linkage or communicator with persons who are outside the family. When strictly enforced, this practice enhances the parent's power position and increases his or her capacity for abuse of power. The heavy price paid for the isolation is, of course, the family's inability to replenish its energy through stimulation, support, nurturance and enjoyment derived from contacts with the outside world. *Denial.* The parental incest family expends an enormous amount of energy upon denial. On the one hand, negative aspects of internal family functioning must be denied in order to be bearable (e.g., the incestuous child sexual abuse, blurred role boundaries, abuse of power, unmet dependency needs and the like). On the other hand, maintaining isolation requires that the outside world be perceived as hostile and threatening; this, in turn requires denial of its positive and attractive aspects. Gutheil and Avery (1975) vividly describe an incestuous family whose members overused denial in an attempt to prevent the children from leaving the family circle and who portrayed temptations and allure of the outside world as "no bed of roses."

Although useful on a short-term basis, denial is not a very effective coping strategy because it requires increasingly greater amounts of energy to maintain denial in the face of multiple conflicting stimuli which somehow bridge the isolation gap. In addition, constant denial can be destructive to the individual who employs this defense mechanism because it diminishes one's capacity to empathize with others.

Lack of empathy. Inability to empathize with others is a hallmark of the perpetrator of child sexual abuse. This characteristic includes unresponsiveness to another person's feelings at all levels—reactions, fears, needs, and the like. It is not unusual for offenders to report, "I told her to tell me if she wanted me to stop but she never said anything." At the same time, their victims report, "I told him he was hurting me, but he acted like he didn't hear me." Insensitivity to another person's feelings is rooted in denial and in failure or inability to communicate with others. It simplifies abuse of power because failure to perceive the negative consequences of exploitation of the victim diminishes or even eliminates guilt for the perpetrator. Accordingly, a callous disregard for others characterizes most family interactions and constitutes a major family treatment need.

Poor communication patterns. Members of parental incest families do not communicate well with each other or with outsiders. Poor communication patterns tend to be the rule, rather than the exception. When weaker family members are exploited by more powerful relatives, they learn that power and control are all-important and greatly to be desired and sought after. Experiencing this harsh reality undermines the credibility of the parents' verbal communication of societal rules regarding inter-personal interaction. The family's isolation also tends to decrease opportunities for children to practice communication skills. Denial and lack of empathy both contribute to poor communication and failure to communicate. Refusal to communicate is also one way for individuals who occupy power positions to consolidate their power base by catching others off guard. Alternatively, less powerful family members may retaliate by refusal to communicate as well. The need to improve communication patterns must be addressed in effective family treatment for parental incest.

Inadequate controls and limit-setting. Persons who occupy power positions in parental incest families tend to have poor impulse control and to fail to set realistic limits upon themselves and others. They may find it difficult to delay gratification of their own needs and desires and depend upon abuse of power to try to meet these needs. At the same time, they tend to fear their own impulsive tendencies and to project them upon others. Hence the inappropriate limit setting: sometimes the limits imposed by persons in power for themselves and others will be harsh and unrealistic. The setting of inappropriate limits invites the breaching of those limits. If imposed limits are breached with impunity, family members may feel both guilty and angry: guilty because of fear of authority; angry because a person in power abused power by failing to abide by established limits. This characteristic of parental incest families is closely related to blurred boundaries and extreme deprivation and neediness.

Blurred boundaries. Inadequate controls and limit-setting invite a blurring of role boundaries and role confusion in parental incest families. The boundaries that pertain are both physical and emotional. Physical boundaries are ignored whenever a powerful person abuses power by observing or touching a weaker person inappropriately. The blurring of physical boundaries can extend to demanding access to the victim's body, belongings, time in the bathroom and bedroom and personal space. Such blurring of physical boundaries may co-exist with rigid expressed limits for all family members— limits which are nevertheless breached by powerful persons whenever they wish.

Blurring of physical boundaries coexists with blurring of emotional boundaries in parental incest families. The parent or parent figure is not likely to breach physical boundaries unless he or she has an inadequate perception of the victim's role as well as his or her own role. By definition an adult's choice to turn to a child for gratification of the adult's needs constitutes role confusion. A resultant blurring of role boundaries and role confusion is inevitable for the child victim and the youngster's behavior thereafter may well compound the problem. As the child's behavior in an inappropriate role persists, the problem of blurring the role boundaries and role confusion is increased for the entire family. All such behavior tends to be self-reinforcing and so the underlying problem becomes worse over time.

Extreme emotional deprivation and neediness. All human beings have dependency needs which must be gratified in order for normal growth and development to occur. Infants are totally helpless and their obvious physical needs for food, warmth and bodily care coexist with equally significant emotional needs. If the physical needs are not met satisfactorily, the child will die or fail to develop normally in a physical sense. Inadequate gratification of the emotional need to be cared for consistently by nurturing humans may also result in death in infancy. However, marginal gratification of essential emotional needs in early childhood combined with adequate gratification of physical needs tend to produce persons who experience extreme neediness and deprivation throughout their lives. Under conditions which pre-dispose to optimal growth and development, children learn how to meet normal dependency needs in ways that are constructive and healthy. These patterns of healthy need gratification persist into adulthood and are likely to be conveyed to one's own children. Conversely, persons with exaggerated dependency needs tend to seek gratification in ways that are pathological and destructive. In addition to a life-long pattern of failing to satisfy their own needs adequately, such persons tend to reproduce themselves in a psychosocial sense: i.e., they teach these dysfunctional patterns to their own children as well as encourage dysfunctional patterns of need gratification in their spouses and in others within their family and social circles.

Magical expectations. Individuals who are extremely needy and emotionally deprived tend to have magical expectations of other people and the world in which they live. Extremely needy persons look around them and perceive that at least some other people around them appear satisfied with themselves and with their surroundings. Presumably these satisfied people have appropriate sources of need gratification. In contrast, the infantile level of emotional deprivation which characterized parents or parent figures in the incestuous family encourages them to select inappropriate choices for need gratification. Implicit in these choices is a magical expectation that this time, in this way, by some unknown means or method, their needs will finally be met.

Repeated failures to meet basic needs via inappropriate choices for need gratification simply reinforces the belief that somewhere an elusive and magical solution exists; surely it *must* exist, for how else do others manage to feel happy and fulfilled? The incestuous parent or parent figure engages a child in sexual activity for the purpose of gratifying non-sexual needs. When parental incest is disclosed, it may be inferred that the dysfunctional and destructive aspects of this form of need gratification in some way outweighed whatever benefits or gains that were derived for the offender, the victim and the family.

Magical expectations tend to characterize all members of the incestuous family, practically without exception. The offending parent exercises magical expectations by selecting a child to gratify his or her non-sexual needs via sexual expression. Other adult family members contribute to the pattern of magical expectations either by directly encouraging the inappropriate sexual relationship between the adult and the child or else by failing to perceive it while still tolerating a variety of infringements of role boundaries and permitting role confusion to take place. The victim, hampered by a life-long indoctrination, has had ample opportunity to absorb a distorted perception of how the world really works. With constant reinforcement from authority figures at home that "rain falls up instead of down," small wonder that the child may eventually disclose the incest secret to an outsider, hoping for what is probably a totally unrealistic consequence of the disclosure.

Magical expectations cannot be overcome without addressing the extreme neediness and emotional deprivation of those who hold them. The latter becomes a primary treatment issue for the parental incest family, as described in the next section.

Treatment Approaches in Parental Incest

Needless to say, those who would treat parental incest families must employ strategies for working with involuntary clients, be prepared to offer total life support and be willing to use the incestuous child sexual abuse to force powerful family members to address their actual treatment needs. As previously stated, individual and group treatment modalities must be used in conjunction with family therapy. If not, family therapy with an individual therapist is liable to have one of two results. Either the powerful family members will attempt to enlist the inwitting aid of the therapist to deny the sexual abuse, to avoid accountability, to maintain their positions of power which enable them to abuse power and to maintain all of the internal family pathology or else they will drop out of treatment when confronted by the therapist who insists upon holding them accountable and addressing the real treatment issues. The former result reinforces family pathology and manipulates the family therapy sessions into a reenactment of the pathological inter-relationships already present. The latter result effectively ends family treatment and sometimes also either ends or subverts victim treatment. Sometimes, powerful family members who drop out of treatment will compromise by allowing the child to remain in treatment, thereby identifying him or her as the problem. Unfortunately, unless the therapist is vigilant, they may still undermine and sabotage treatment for the child who remains at home.

What will work for these families? Several treatment modalities must be employed simultaneously. Individual, dyad, group, couples, and family therapy can all be used in some combination. Group therapy (e.g., fathers group, mothers group, parents group, adolescent group), permits both peer support and confrontation—essential elements of treatment that are difficult to reproduce in individual therapy. Arts therapies (including play therapy) will be invaluable, especially for the more damaged and less expressive family members.

All family treatment must address the underlying family treatment needs. Appropriate use of power, reconciliation of authority conflicts, affiliation rather than isolation, decreased reliance upon denial as a coping mechanism, heightened sensitivity of others' needs, improved communication patterns, adequate controls and limit setting, establishment and maintenance of appropriate boundaries, acceptable need gratification and development of realistic expectations—all are necessary treatment goals for the parental incest family. In addition to holding them accountable for child sexual abuse, therapist(s) must help adults in parental incest families to recognize and avoid high risk situations. Although it is important for the adult clients to acknowledge their responsibility for the incestuous child sexual abuse, saying the words and "getting in touch with feelings" is not enough. Actions must show that child sexual abuse has stopped. To accomplish this end, it is extremely important to define the family's problems as clearly as possible, to decide which problems will be addressed by the treatment program, and to formulate a treatment plan to address the problems as specifically as possible.

REFERENCES

Anderson, L. M. & Shafer, G. The Character-Disordered Family: A Community Treatment Model for Family Sexual Abuse, *American Journal of Orthopsychiatry*, 1979, 49 (3).

Beavers, W. R. A Theoretical Basis for Family Evaluation, In J. M. Lewis (ed.), *No Single Thread: Psychological Health in Family Systems*. New York: Brunner-Mazel, 1976.

Burgess, A. W. and Holmstrom, L. L. *Rape: Crisis and Recovery*, Robert T. Brady Company, 1979 Bowie, Maryland.

Burgess, A. W., Holmstrom, L. L., McCauseland, M. P. Child Sexual Assault by Family Member, *Victimology: An International Journal*, 1977, 2, 236–250.

Groth, A. N. & Burgess, A. W. Motivational Intent in the Sexual Assault of Children, *Criminal Justice and Behavior:* 1977, 4, 253–264.

Gutheil, T. B. and Avery N. C. Multiple Overt Incest as Family Defense Against Loss, *Family Process.* 1975, (661), pp. 105–116.

Kempe, H. C. Sexual Abuse: Another Hidden Pediatric Problem, 1977 C. Anderson Aldrich Lecture.

Laury, G. V. How Parents May Unwittingly Sexually Abuse Their Children, *Behavioral Medicine,* February, 1978, pp. 33–35.

Poznanski, E. and Blos, P. Incest, *Medical Aspects of Human Sexuality,* October, 1975, pp. 46–76.

Sgroi, S. M. *A Handbook of Clinical Intervention in Child Sexual Abuse,* Lexington, Massachusetts: Lexington Books, 1982.

THE CHILD MOLESTER: CLINICAL OBSERVATIONS

A. Nicholas Groth, PhD
William F. Hobson, MS
Thomas S. Gary, MEd

Introduction

An increasing amount of attention is being focused on the sexual victimization of children, yet no exact statistics exist in regard to this problem for a number of reasons: Many such victimizations may go unreported or undetected, or the suspect may not be apprehended; or there may be insufficient evidence to go to court; or the offender is not convicted; or even if he is convicted his offense may fall under a number of different statutes which are not age-specific—in Massachusetts, for example, the sexual victimization of a child can be encompassed under 25 different statutes—and therefore it is impossible to retrieve the number of identified sexual offenses committed specifically against children. Nevertheless human service and criminal justice professionals are encountering more and more reported incidents of inter-generation sexual activity. The authors of this chapter are clinicians who have worked with identified sexual offenders against children in a variety of institutional and community-based settings. Our professional experience to date has spanned 16 years and encompassed over 500 such offenders, and our aim in this chapter is to share our clinical observations, ideas, and impressions derived from our work in the hope that this will offer others a useful overview and approach to understanding and working with the child molester. Our sample of identified offenders may be biased—there may be better integrated individuals who commit similar offenses with more discretion and circumspection and thus remain undetected—but our offenders have in fact encompassed a sufficiently broad spectrum in regard to age, education, and occupation to persuade us that the fact of identification and conviction is not a distorting variable with regard to the psychology of the child offender. With increasing opportunity to work with and study such offenders our knowledge of the offender, his offense, and his victim continues to develop, and we find that many of the commonly held assumptions in regard to the child molester (pedophile) are not being substantiated.

Myths About Child Molestation

Generally in order to safeguard children against sexual victimization, they are admonished to watch out for advances from strangers. For the most part, however, the child molester is not a stranger, the large majority being in fact known and often related to their victims. The child molester is commonly stereotyped as a "dirty old man" or a "monster." The fact is that in more than half the cases we have worked with we found that the offender had attempted or committed his first sexual assault by the age of 16. Although most identified offenders are adults this only reflects the point at which their behavior is recognized as an offense, not the onset of their sexual pathology. Because the sexual victimization of children is so reprehensible, the offender is perceived to be some sort of depraved monster. Again in our experience we have by and large not found this to be the case. His offense has been more the product of immaturity than malicious intent, and in many respects the offender may otherwise be living a competent, law-abiding, and productive life. Unfortunately, when people expect the offender to be a monster and the accused is a respectable person, then doubt is shed on the veracity of the victim's allegations—the child is thought to be mistaken or even lying. Generally speaking we have not found any social or demographic characteristics that differentiate the child molester from the general population, not his race, religion, intelligence, education, vocation, socio-economic class, or the like. What we have found is that pedophilia cuts across the whole spectrum of diagnostic categories, but for the most part we are not dealing with persons who are mentally ill but who are emotionally troubled. The defects in their functioning are not cognitive, or perceptual, or emotional, but interpersonal. What we are dealing with, in most cases, is the aftermath of physical and/or psychological abuse, neglect, exploitation, and/or abandonment during the offender's formative years which has precluded the development of a sense of relatedness to others.

We have also observed that alcohol and drug abuse play a relatively minor role in the commission of such offenses, that females as well as males sexually molest children although such offenses are less socially visible and under-reported, that preadolescent boys and girls are at equal risk of being sexually victimized, and that men who sexually molest boys are misidentified as homosexuals when they are in fact pedophiles.

Finally the child molester is the recipient of the strongest societal anger and disapproval which ironically only confirms his perception of adults as hostile and punitive and reinforces his attraction to children. If we are genuinely concerned about combatting the sexual victimization of children we must be humanistic in our attitudes towards the offender so that we don't inadvertantly perpetuate the problem. If part of the reason the offender turns to children is because he is intimidated by adults and he is then placed in a prison setting which exposes him to threats of harm, humiliation, exploitation, and physical abuse at the hands of other inmates, this may serve only to reinforce his fear, distrust, and avoidance of adults and to encourage his seeking out children whom he perceives will not hate or hurt him. Where incarceration is required, then, a security treatment center specifically for sex offenders is preferable to a conventional correctional institution or prison.

The Offense

What is child sexual victimization? It is any behavior on the part of an individual that exposes a child to the risk of psychological interference in his or her sexual development. The spectrum of such victimization may range from situations at one extreme in which there is no direct physical contact with the victim (for example, the offender may expose himself or he may encourage children to permit him to photograph them in the nude) to those at the other extreme in which the child may be physically attacked and injured or even killed. Sexual offenses against children can be classified into two basic categories in regard to the mode of aggression exhibited in the offense: child molesters and child rapists. Some offenders gain sexual access to the child through a combination of enticement and deception. They lure or trick the child into the sexual activity; reward the child for his or her participation; and caution the child against disclosure. These non-violent offenders, whom we refer to as *child molesters,* essentially coax or pressure the child into the sexual activity. Their offenses constitute sexual extortion in which the child is taught to provide sex in exchange for attention, acceptance, recognition, and material gain. Other offenders resort to threat, intimidation, and physical force to achieve submission on the part of the victim. Thcy are *child rapists* who overpower and/or threaten to harm their victims. Their offenses constitute sexual attacks in which the child victim relinquishes sex in return for survival and release. Obviously the child rapist poses a more serious risk to the physical safety of the victim than does the child molester, but fortunately child rapists constitute a small minority of the sexual offenders against children. For this reason the remainder of this chapter will focus on the major type of perpetrator of sexual offenses against children: the child molester.

Definition

What is a child molester? As it is used in this chapter, the term "child-molester" refers to a significantly older person whose conscious sexual interests and overt sexual behaviors are directed either partially or exclusively towards prepubertal children. In contrast to the child rapist for whom sexual aggression is a hostile act, the child-molester exhibits a positive emotional investment in the child which he eroticizes. He seeks to establish an on-going relationship with the child which includes but extends beyond sexual activity. Having first established a non-sexual relationship and position of familiarity with the child he gradually indoctrinates the child into sexual activities which become more advanced over time. He behaves in counter-aggressive ways, however, and should the child refuse or resist his sexual advances, the child molester may increase his efforts at enticement and manipulation but will not resort to physical force. If the child actively and persistently resists the child molester will ultimately turn to another, more accommodating victim. The risk to the victim of the child-molester, then, is not one of physical injury, but one of psychological harm.

Typology

One of the most basic observations that can be made about child offenders is that they are not all alike, and our aim in this chapter is to differentiate among various patterns of pedophilic behavior and to identify different types of child molesters. Sexual offenders against children can be divided into two basic types on the basis of their level of socio-sexual maturation: (1) the *fixated* offender whose primary sexual orientation is towards children, and (2) the *regressed* offender whose sexual involvement with a child is a clear departure, under stress, from a primary sexual orientation towards agemates. (See Table 1.)

Fixated Child Molester

For one type of offender his sexual attraction to children constitutes an arrestment of his sociosexual maturation resulting from unresolved formative issues which undermined his subsequent development and persist in his personality functioning. Such an offender exhibits a compulsive attraction to and sexual fixation on children. From the onset of his adolescence children have been the primary or exclusive object of his sexual interests and any sexual contact with age mates that occurs is usually situational in nature, initiated by the other individual involved, and never replaces his preference for and chronic sexual involvement with children.

Clinical Example of a Fixated Offender

Scott is a 20 year old, white, single male of average intelligence who is the product of alcoholic parents and an abusive home. He became aware of his sexual attraction to preadolescent boys when he himself was 13 years old. Scott would sexually approach neighborhood children and engage them in mutual fondling, masturbation, and fellatio: "I would run around making every kid in sight— anyone younger than I was. I'd talk them into it. I'd masturbate just looking at a boy, or fondle him, play with his ass, kiss him, and blow him. I enjoyed being with younger kids." When he was 17 Scott left home and earned a living as a male prostitute and model for pornographic films. In this activity he would engage in sexual relations with adult males and on a few occasions with adult females, but although he would perform sexually with adults and agemates for money, he never experienced being sexually attracted to men or women and found himself "turned-on" only to boys between the ages of 10 and 12.

TABLE 1: TYPOLOGY OF CHILD MOLESTERS

FIXATED TYPE

1. PRIMARY SEXUAL ORIENTATION IS TO CHILDREN.

2. PEDOPHILIC INTERESTS BEGIN AT ADOLESCENCE.

3. NO PRECIPITATING STRESS/NO SUBJECTIVE DISTRESS.

4. PERSISTENT INTEREST AND COMPULSIVE BEHAVIOR.

5. PREMEDITATED, PRE-PLANNED OFFENSES.

6. IDENTIFICATION: OFFENDER IDENTIFIES CLOSELY WITH THE VICTIM AND EQUALIZES HIS BEHAVIOR TO THE LEVEL OF THE CHILD AND/OR MAY ADOPT A PSEUDO-PARENTAL ROLE TO THE VICTIM.

7. MALE VICTIMS ARE PRIMARY TARGETS.

8. LITTLE OR NO SEXUAL CONTACT INITIATED WITH AGEMATES; OFFENDER IS USUALLY SINGLE OR IN A MARRIAGE OF CONVENIENCE.

9. USUALLY NO HISTORY OF ALCOHOL OR DRUG ABUSE AND OFFENSE IS NOT ALCOHOL RELATED.

10. CHARACTEROLOGICAL IMMATURITY; POOR SOCIOSEXUAL PEER RELATIONSHIPS.

11. OFFENSE = MALADAPTIVE RESOLUTION OF LIFE DEVELOPMENT (MATURATION) ISSUES.

REGRESSED TYPE

1. PRIMARY SEXUAL ORIENTATION IS TO AGEMATES.

2. PEDOPHILIC INTERESTS EMERGE IN ADULTHOOD.

3. PRECIPITATING STRESS USUALLY EVIDENT.

4. INVOLVEMENTS MAY BE MORE EPISODIC AND MAY WAX AND WANE WITH STRESS.

5. INITIAL OFFENSE MAY BE IMPULSIVE AND NOT PREMEDITATED.

6. SUBSTITUTION: OFFENDER REPLACES CONFLICTUAL ADULT RELATIONSHIP WITH INVOLVEMENT WITH A CHILD; VICTIM IS A PSEUDOADULT SUBSTITUTE AND IN INCEST SITUATIONS THE OFFENDER ABANDONS HIS PARENTAL ROLE.

7. FEMALE VICTIMS ARE PRIMARY TARGETS.

8. SEXUAL CONTACT WITH A CHILD COEXISTS WITH SEXUAL CONTACT WITH AGEMATES; OFFENDER IS USUALLY MARRIED OR COMMON-LAW.

9. OFFENSE IS OFTEN ALCOHOL RELATED.

10. MORE TRADITIONAL LIFESTYLE BUT UNDER-DEVELOPED PEER RELATIONSHIPS.

11. OFFENSE = MALADAPTIVE ATTEMPT TO COPE WITH SPECIFIC LIFE STRESSES.

Regressed Child Molester

For another type of offender his sexual involvement with a child constitutes a temporary or permanent departure from his more characteristic attraction to age mates. Such a regressed offender did not previously exhibit any predominant sexual interest in significantly younger persons (during his formative years) but when he entered adulthood and experienced the attendant responsibilities and life-demands as overwhelming and/or when his adult relationships became conflictual and emotionally unfulfilling a sexual attraction to children emerged. Such cross-generational sexual activity is typically activated by some precipitating stress and may wax and wane in response to the amount of stress the offender experiences in coping with adult life demands.

Clinical Example of a Regressed Offender

Brad is a 37 year old, white, married male of average intelligence. He reports a fairly unremarkable life history. He had no difficulty in school and feels he grew up in a basically stable home. His sexual development does not appear unconventional. As a child he engaged in sexual play and experimentation with his siblings. He began masturbating at age 15 and experienced intercourse at age 19 with a girlfriend he ultimately married. He reports no extra-marital affairs, but became sexually involved with his 11 year old daughter when he lost his job and discovered that his wife had a terminal illness. Under the pressure of mounting medical bills and other responsibilities Brad began drinking heavily. He states "I loved my wife and children and still and always will. I don't know how this happened. There were times I would get into a deep depression and one day I came home and my daughter was asleep on my bed. That's how it began. At first I just touched her but later I started having intercourse with her." Brad's sexual activity continued for two years during which time he did not engage in sexual activities with persons his own age.

Dynamics

Cross-generational sexual behavior, then, may constitute a fixation on the part of the offender: a sexual orientation towards children as the result of arrested socio-sexual development; or it may constitute a regression, the result of a sudden or progressive deterioration of emotionally meaningful or gratifying adult relation-ships. In general, fixated child molesters are drawn to children sexually in that they identify with the child and appear in some ways to want to remain children themselves. It is for this reason that the trend for fixated offenders is to target boys as victims. This does not represent a homosexual object-choice, psychologi-cally, but a narcissistic one. They see the boy as a projected repre-sentation of themselves. They feel themselves to be more child than adult—more boys than men—and therefore find themselves more comfortable (especially sexually) in the company of children (boys/girls) than adults (men/women).

Regressed child molesters turn to a child sexually as a substitute for their adult relationships which have become conflictual and emotionally unfulfilling. Since most such offenders are primarily emotionally invested in women in their adult relationships, it is for this reason that the trend for regressed child molesters is to target girls as victims. They select a child (girl), with whom they will feel more competent, to replace the adult (woman) with whom they feel inadequate.

The psychological basis of pedophilia, then, is feelings of inade-quacy, immaturity, vulnerability, helplessness, and isolation. Adult sexuality is threatening and, consequently, is avoided or abandoned. The child molester instead relates to a child as if the child were a peer or equal. The fixated offender does this by adapting his inter-ests and behavior to the level of the child, whereas the regressed offender relates to the child as if she or he were an adult. Psycho-logically the fixated offender experiences himself as a child, whereas the regressed offender experiences the child as a pseudo-adult. For both the victim represents a fantasy. The level of the offender's socio-sexual maturation can be gauged from the age of the victim he characteristically selects.

Motivations

What prompts an adult to become sexually involved with a child? Pedophilia is complex and multi-determined. Sexual involvement with a child is by definition coercive on the part of the adult, since the child does not occupy equal power status to the adult. By virtue of being an adult the grownup possesses social authority, physical superiority, wider experience, and greater knowledge than the child.

In sexual encounters with adults children may cooperate but they are not capable of giving informed consent. For this reason pedophilia constitutes the sexual abuse of power. As with other forms of sexual assault (rape, indecent exposure, obscene telephone calling, and the like), sexual desire or passion does not appear to be the primary determinant of such behavior. Child molestation is the sexual expression of non-sexual needs and unresolved life issues. Pedophilia goes beyond sexual need and is, ultimately, a pseudo-sexual act.

Through sexual involvement with a child the offender attempts to fulfill his psychological needs for recognition, acceptance, validation, affiliation, mastery, and control. It is not sexual gratification or release, per se, that is the source of the satisfaction the offender finds in his sexual contact with the victim; it is his interpretation of the sexual activity as evidence of the child's acceptance and caring about him. "She was glad to see me;" "He looked up to me;" "She loved me;" "He made me feel important;" are typical comments made by the offender in regard to his victim. In addition he feels more in control in a relationship to a child where there is less risk of an emotionally devastating rebuff or rejection. Nor is his sense of competency threatened by a child who is more accepting and less demanding than an adult.

Intimidated by adult sexuality, the child-molester withdraws to pre-sexual or non-sexual children, typically describing the appeal of children as their being innocent, loving, open, warm, trusting, and clean. Sex is "dirty" and pre-adolescent children are sexless—that is, they do not confront the offender with physical characteristics of adult sexuality: the boy's genitals are small, he does not ejaculate, his body is smooth and hairless; the girl likewise has no pubic hair or breast development, she does not menstruate, she cannot become pregnant. It may seem to be a paradox that the child molester is sexually attracted to a non-sexual person, but it is not a paradox when it is realized that the primary motivation underlying such offenses is not sexual.

It is through the sexual activity with a child that the offender attempts to solve unresolved issues of his development and fulfill unmet needs in his life. It is for this reason that the child molester typically seeks on-going sexual involvement with his victim. He is searching through sex for something that goes beyond sex. Since such sexual behavior cannot ultimately resolve the underlying issues nor meet the unfulfilled needs, it becomes repetitive or compulsive in nature—both self-perpetuating and self-defeating at the same time—and in this respect is equivalent to symptom-formation. Just as an alcoholic is not driven to drink out of thirst, a pedophile is not molesting children simply out of sexual desire.

Generally speaking, the clinical impression that emerges in regard to a child molester is that of an immature individual whose pedophilic behavior serves to compensate for his relative helplessness in meeting adult bio-psycho-social life demands. It offers him a retreat from conflictual adult relationships. It provides a sense of power, control, and competence. It fulfills a longing for intimacy, affection, and affiliation. It validates his worth. And it may provide some sexual gratification. However, all of this is basically illusionary and transient. The child will eventually mature and the offender must then find another victim.

Symptom Choice

Why does an individual become sexually drawn to children? Why is pedophilia the symptom that emerges in response to psychological stress? Again, such complex behavior cannot be reduced to a single cause. It may be the product of a number of incompletely understood bio-psycho-social variables, yet the role of sexual victimization in the developmental histories of child molesters appears to be a significant factor. The majority of child molesters that we have worked with have themselves been sexually abused children, and just as the battered child runs a high risk of becoming a battering parent, so too, it appears, does the sexually victimized child—especially the male—run a high risk of becoming a sexual victimizer. Pedophilia, then, may reflect yet another dynamic: an attempt to resolve an unresolved sexual trauma. One way in which the male child may try to combat the feelings of powerlessness inherent in being a victim is to ultimately identify with the aggressor and reverse roles; that is, to become the powerful victimizer rather than the helpless victim. The child molester then re-enacts in his offense the characteristics of his own victimization in an attempt to restore to himself a feeling of being in control. To combat the negative feelings associated with his own victimization he attempts to "romanticize" his sexual offense and regard it as an expression of his caring for the child victim rather than his using the child to meet his own needs (a fact suggested by his emotional over-investment in the child).

It appears to be an inescapable conclusion that pedophilia is one of the possible consequences of child sexual abuse and neglect. For this reason, when working with offenders, it is important to carefully explore what was occurring in their lives especially at the time they were the same age as the child they are victimizing.

Treatment

Treatment may be defined as any type of intervention designed to reduce, prevent, or eliminate the risk of the child molester again committing an offense. To achieve this requires effecting changes in the internal psychological predisposition of the offender; in his external living environment; or in both. Essentially, the goal is one of control: either the offender must develop (internal) control over his pedophilic behavior or he must be (externally) controlled so as to prevent his acting out such interests. There are four basic treatment modalities aimed at developing controls over pedophilic urges:

1. *Chemotherapy.* Various antiandrogenic hormones, such as Depo-Provera, have been shown to have a moderating effect on sexual aggressiveness and enhance self-regulation of sexual behavior. Although the use of Depo-Provera in the treatment of sexual offenders is still in the experimental stages, it does offer promise as a chemical control of antisocial sexual behaviors such as pedophilia.
2. *Behavior Modification.* Another approach in working with child offenders is to address the specific behaviors associated with the offense and, through a series of conditioning exercises based on learning principles, to diminish sexual arousal to children and enhance sexual responsiveness to adults. Progress is monitored by physiological measurements of erection responses to relevant stimuli. This modality attempts to change the clients' sexual preferences by making aversive those sexual behaviors which are outlawed and by replacing them with more socially acceptable sexual behaviors.
3. *Psychotherapy.* This modality encompasses a wide range of approaches based on interpersonal interaction and views the offending sexual behavior as symptomatic of internal emo-

tional conflicts which can be resolved through achieving awareness and better understanding of the underlying issues. Through such introspection the offender is expected to arrive at better controls over his sexually inappropriate behavior.

4. *Psychosocial education.* This modality, which we employ at our facility, views sexual offenses to be the products of defects in human development and attempts to remedy such defects through a combination of re-education, resocialization, and counseling. The aim is to alert the offender to the life issues that stress him, to either find ways of avoiding such stresses or develop life management skills to better cope with such demands; and to self-observe and recognize characteristic early behaviors or warning signals that indicate he is moving towards a repetition of his offense. Table 2 provides an overview of psychoeducational services regularly provided to inmates at the Connecticut Correctional Institution at Somers.

Rehabilitation

It would be misleading to suggest that we have reached a state of clinical knowledge that insures the successful rehabilitation of adults who sexually molest children. As yet, no single method of treatment or type of therapeutic intervention has proved to be a totally effective remedy. And given the wide range of individual differences found among child molesters, it is unlikely that any single treatment will ever prove suitable for all such offenders. Treatment has to be tailored to the specific needs and abilities of the individual client. Since, by definition, a sexual assault is an interpersonal act involving sexuality and aggression, at a minimum these three major issues (aggression, sexuality, and interpersonal relations) must be addressed in any program of treatment or rehabilitation.

In working with involuntary clients, treatment is necessarily compulsory and traditional approaches must be adapted or modified for this client. This includes exercising power over the client in a responsible fashion, confronting and controlling him, doing persistent outreach and monitoring, providing concrete support services, anticipating the guidance he needs, and implementing the consequences or penalities for failure to fulfill the conditions of treatment.

Our expectations of clients in treatment are that they will come to recognize their problems through knowledge of their symptoms, ad-

TABLE 2: APPLICATION FORM, SEX OFFENDER PROGRAM, CONNECTICUT CORRECTIONAL INSTITUTION-SOMERS

INDICATE YOUR CHOICES AND THEIR ORDER OF PREFERENCE:

1. ( ) REGULAR GROUP THERAPY. (MEMBERS WITHIN THE SAME GROUP WILL ALL HAVE COMMITTED
A SIMILAR TYPE OF OFFENSE. DISCUSSION WILL FOCUS ON
YOUR OFFENSE AND THE UNDERLYING ISSUES RELATED TO IT.)

2. ( ) SEX EDUCATION. (A BASIC INTRODUCTION TO HUMAN SEXUALITY. DISCUSSION WILL FOCUS
ON MYTHS ABOUT SEX, COMMOM QUESTIONS AND CONCERNS, VARIATIONS IN
SEXUAL BEHAVIOR, VALUES AND ATTITUDES. ATTENTION WILL BE GIVEN TO SEXUAL ROLES,
GENDER AND IDENTITY ISSUES, COMMUNICATION PROBLEMS, REPRODUCTION, ETC.)

3. ( ) RELATIONSHIPS TO WOMEN. (DISCUSSION WILL FOCUS ON CONCERNS AND PROBLEMS
EXPERIENCED IN RELATING TO WOMEN. ATTENTION WILL BE
GIVEN TO ATTITUDES TOWARD WOMEN, EXPECTATIONS IN REGARD TO WOMEN, AND AN
UNDERSTANDING OF WOMEN'S ISSUES.)

4. ( ) PERSONAL VICTIMIZATION. (DISCUSSION WILL FOCUS ON CONCERNS AND PROBLEMS EXPERIENCED
IN REGARD TO HAVING BEEN A VICTIM OF ABUSE, TRAUMA, OR
EXPLOITATION AS A YOUNGSTER OR YOUNG ADULT. ATTENTION WILL BE GIVEN TO BETTER
UNDERSTAND ONE'S SEXUAL AND AGGRESSIVE ATTITUDES, VALUES, FANTASIES, AND THE LIKE,
AS WELL AS TO CONCERNS AND PROBLEMS EXPERIENCED IN REGARD TO SEXUAL DEVELOPMENT.)

5. ( ) UNDERSTANDING SEXUAL ASSAULT. (DISCUSSION WILL FOCUS ON THE DYNAMICS OF SEXUAL
OFFENSES, PATTERNS OF ASSAULT, THE PSYCHOLOGY OF
THE OFFENDER, CLINICAL ASPECTS OF SEXUAL ASSAULT, TREATMENT APPROACHES, ETC.)

6. ( ) VICTIM PERSONALIZATION. (DISCUSSION WILL FOCUS ON THE IMPACT OF VARIOUS TYPES OF
SEXUAL OFFENSES ON THE VICTIM. ATTENTION WILL BE GIVEN
TO THE AFTEREFFECTS OF SEXUAL ASSAULT ON VICTIMS, BOTH MALE AND FEMALE, ADULT AND
CHILD. THIS GROUP WILL HELP THE OFFENDER TO MORE FULLY UNDERSTAND APPRECIATE WHY
VICTIMS BEHAVE AS THEY DO AND HOW THEIR LIVES ARE AFFECTED BY BEING VICTIMIZED.)

7. ( ) MANAGEMENT OF ANGER AND AGGRESSION. (DISCUSSION WILL FOCUS ON DIFFICULTIES IN REGARD
TO AGGRESSION MANAGEMENT, SUCH AS HAVING A
PROBLEM WITH ONE'S TEMPER, OR GETTING INVOLVED IN HIGH RISK ACTIVITIES FOR EXCITEMENT,
AND ON EFFORTS TO BETTER HANDLE THESE FEELINGS. ATTENTION WILL BE GIVEN TO WAYS OF
BEING ASSERTIVE WITHOUT BEING AGGRESSIVE AND TO THE UNDERLYING REASONS RELATED TO
ANGER AND AGGRESSION.)

8. ( ) SOCIODRAMA/COMMUNICATION SKILLS. (THIS GROUP WILL FOCUS ON INTERRELATING AND
COMMUNICATING EFFECTIVELY WITH OTHERS. THROUGH
THE USE OF ROLE-PLAYING AND VIDEO-TAPING PARTICIPANTS WILL BE ABLE TO IMPROVE
THEIR EMPATHY, SOCIAL SKILLS, AND COMMUNICATIONS IN DEALING WITH LIFE SITUATIONS
INVOLVING OTHER PEOPLE.)

9. ( ) COMBATTING SEXUAL ASSAULT. (AT VARIOUS TIMES THROUGHOUT THE YEAR DIFFERENT PEOPLE
WHO ARE CONCERNED ABOUT SEXUAL ASSAULT AND INTERESTED
IN LEARNING MORE ABOUT THE SEXUAL OFFENDER WILL VISIT THE SEX OFFENDER PROGRAM AT
CCI-SOMERS. THEY MAY BE STUDENTS, VICTIM COUNSELORS, LAW ENFORCEMENT OFFICERS,
NURSES, THERAPISTS, AND THE LIKE, WHOSE WORK BRINGS THEM INTO CONTACT WITH THE
VICTIM OF SEXUAL ASSAULT, THE OFFENDER, OR BOTH. YOUR KNOWLEDGE AND EXPERIENCE
CAN CONTRIBUTE TO THEIR UNDERSTANDING AND EDUCATION.)

10. ( ) PARENTS ANONYMOUS. (PARTICIPATION IN THIS GROUP IS LIMITED TO MEN WHO ARE PARENTS
OR ARE IN A PARENTING RELATIONSHIP WITH ONE OR MORE CHILDREN.
PARENTS ANONYMOUS OPERATES ON THE SELF-HELP, MUTUAL-AID CONCEPT OR MODEL. MEMBERS
OF THE GROUP SET AGENDA AND DECIDE HOW THEY WISH TO USE GROUP TIME. MAJOR ISSUES
TO BE DEALT WITH INCLUDE HOW TO BE AN EFFECTIVE PARENT, HOW TO RELATE TO CHILDREN
APPROPRIATELY, ETC.)

11. ( ) DEALING WITH ANXIETY AND TENSION: BIOFEEDBACK. (FOCUS IS ON LEARNING TO RELAX AND
RELIEVE TENSION THROUGH AN
INDIVIDUAL BIOFEEDBACK PROCESS. THE INMATE USES A SERIES OF INSTRUCTIONAL TAPES
THAT TEACH HIM STRESS REDUCTION AND RELAXATION TECHNIQUES AND MEASURES HIS PROGRESS
ON A BIOFEEDBACK MACHINE.)

* * *

mit to their behavior, see it as inappropriate, realize it is compulsive behavior over which they must gain control, accept responsibility for what they have done, and make amendments. Basically, treatment is coercive—the offender, realizing the social and legal consequences of disclosure does not self-refer. Therefore, treatment must be confrontative. The client needs to be told that he has a problem and needs help and told where to get help.

Essentially there are two basic options in regard to disposition of child molestation cases: 1. the offender may be incarcerated or 2. the offender may be referred to an outpatient program or agency for treatment. In our view the latter should always be stipulated as a condition of probation or parole.

Disposition Guidelines

In the assessment of the offender we find treatment in an outpatient setting counterindicated when:

a. the threat of harm or actual physical force or abuse played a role in the offense,
b. the sexual activity involved any bizarre or ritualistic acts (such as enemas or bondage),
c. the sexual offense is one aspect of numerous antisocial behaviors or a criminal lifestyle,
d. the sexual offense is secondary to a condition of serious psychopathology (such as psychosis, retardation, addiction, or organicity),
e. the offense constitutes a chronic sexual fixation on children rather than a regression under identifiable stresses,
f. the offender either denies his offense or does not regard such behavior as inappropriate and there is no dependable agent to supervise or monitor his daily living,
g. the offender has few psychological areas of conflict-free functioning and few dependable social and occupational skills to manage most adult demands adequately.

When some or most of the above conditions prevail, then the placement of choice is an institutional setting. However, whatever treatment is begun or accomplished in this setting must be continued on an outpatient basis after release.

Since in fact child molesters will be found in a variety of settings—in prisons, in mental hospitals, in residential treatment programs, and in the community—treatment services need to be available in all these settings. Furthermore, since we regard this problem as a chronic one, it is something the offender will need to work on every day of his life and there will need to be support services available to help him—not only professional agencies and programs, but also, and even more important, self-help groups such as Parents Anonymous, Parents United, Alcoholics Anonymous, and the like. Unfortunately, many mental health and social service agencies shy away from treating sexual offenders because of their discomfort over the nature of the behavior or because they feel they lack the expertise to counsel this group of individuals. Some agencies are willing to treat the offender, but do so in traditional ways which are often inappropriate and/or ineffective for this client. They may avoid discussing the actual offense, for example, because they are uncomfortable with the subject, whereas we feel that it is necessary to discuss and directly confront the behavior early on in treatment. Another problem centers around the issue of therapist-client confidentiality. Although confidentiality may be appropriate when treating non-criminal behavior, it is not appropriate when dealing with the child sex offender since it perpetuates the secrecy which is so much a part of the offense itself. The therapist must assume professional responsibility to protect any potential victims of this client.

Summary

One of the crucial factors in combatting the sexual molestation of children is the identification and treatment of the offender. Yet most clinicians are not being trained to work with such clients in the course of their graduate schooling. As a result, offenders continue to be recycled back into the community without the support services necessary to reduce the risk of recidivism. In this chapter, we have attempted to provide an introductory overview of the child molester, to summarize our clinical impressions derived from many years work with such offenders, and to offer some guidelines and suggestions for assessing and treating such referrals. The aim of this chapter is not to provide anything approaching a definitive work on the child offender, but instead to offer a framework for human service providers who come into contact with such clients so as to facilitate their work in dealing with this complex and multidetermined issue.

To effect such treatment requires an inter-agency and multidisciplinary team approach. Child molestation is behavior that crosses clinical, legal, and social boundaries and to effectively combat this serious problem there must be open communication among all who play a role in the management of the offender—the clinician, the court, the parole or probation officer, the victim's counselor, and the like.

SUGGESTED READINGS

Burgess, A.W.; Groth, A.N.; H., L.L.; & Sgroi, S.M. *Sexual Assault of Children and Adolescents,* Lexington: Lexington Books, 1978.

Groth, A.N., with Birnbaum, H.J. *Men Who Rape: The Psychology of the Offender,* New York: Plenum, 1979.

Sanford, L.T. *The Silent Children,* New York: Doubleday, 1980.

Sgroi, S.M. *A Handbook of Clinical Intervention in Child Sexual Abuse,* Lexington: Lexington Books, 1981.

CHILD SEXUAL ABUSE
AND THE COURTS:
PRELIMINARY FINDINGS

Carl M. Rogers, PhD

Sexual victimization of children, including incest, rape, and other forms of sexual molestation, constitutes a social problem of major proportions in the United States. Estimates regarding the incidence of such sexual victimization vary greatly depending upon the study setting, the definitional criteria, and the methodology used for collecting such information. Most studies however would suggest that perhaps 200,000 to 400,000 children are sexually victimized every year in the United States (American Humane Association, 1968; Chaneles, 1967; Gagnon, 1965). Some retrospective studies would suggest that the incidence is higher still with one of every five girls and one of every ten boys (Finkelhor, 1979) or one of every three children (Landis, 1956) being sexually victimized at least once during their childhood.

Sexual victimization of children constitutes a major social problem not only due to its high frequency of occurrence but also due to its overall impact on the child victim and her or his family. Studies suggest that sexual victimization as a child may be related to later difficulties in psychosocial adjustment including drug abuse (Benward & Densen-Gerber, 1976), juvenile delinquency (Halleck, 1962), juvenile prostitution (James & Meyerding, 1977), adult clinical depression (Summit & Kryso, 1978), and similar difficulties. In addition, numerous reports attest to the immediate deleterious psycho-social effects of such victimization on children (e.g., Forward & Buck, 1978; Bach & Anderson, Note 1; Burgess & Holstrom, 1978; Greenberg, 1979; Peters, 1976; etc.).

In addition to the trauma of victimization itself, mental health professionals have become increasingly concerned about the potential for "secondary victimization" of these children as the result of societal intervention efforts. Particular concern has been focused upon the possible negative impact of criminal justice procedures which have been frequently seen as both increasing the degree of emotional distress experienced by the child victim and decreasing the likelihood of either offender conviction or other successful resolution of the problem (cf., Burgess & Holstrom, 1978; Davidson & Bulkley, 1980; Kirkwood & Mihaila, 1979; Stevens & Berliner, 1980).

Although original concerns focused primarily on police and prosecutorial sensitivity in handling of these cases, recent attention has focused upon deficiencies or problems inherent in the adversary nature and constitutional structure of the American criminal justice process, particularly the rights to open confrontation and cross examination of witnesses or complianants in a public hearing (e.g., Davidson and Bulkley, 1980; Libai, 1969). The perceived degree of trauma visited upon the child victim by the court system and constitutional barriers to substantial change of this system have led some legal experts to conclude that, at least in intrafamily cases, court action should be only taken when it can be agreed that the child will emerge from the process better than she entered it and when it is the least detrimental alternative available (Davidson & Bulkley, 1980).

Such a standard for proceeding with court action seems ill-advised. First, it is difficult, if not impossible to predict with any reasonable certainty the impact of the court process on the child victim. Too many factors are beyond the control of the prosecution and unknowable until court action has actually commenced, such as behavior of the defendant during the proceedings, number of defense-requested continuances which will be granted, the style of cross-examination, and so forth. Second, this approach requires consensus between prosecutor, social worker, and other involved professionals—such consensus is difficult to achieve on such a conjectural issue. Third, the standard would suggest that court action would not proceed even when court action would neither help nor hurt the child. Finally, and perhaps most importantly, the approach recommended by Davidson and Bulkley allows little consideration to the wishes of the victim regarding whether to proceed with court action.

Examination of court processing of child sexual abuse cases in the District of Columbia, however, would suggest that while limitations and procedural barriers do exist, the realitiesof criminal justice handling of these cases are not nearly as bleak or detrimental as often portrayed (Conte & Berliner, in press). Cases handled by the Special Unit of the Child Protection Center (CPC-SU) of Children's Hospital National Medical Center (Washington, D. C.) since early 1978 have been followed as they progress within the legal/judicial system. Preliminary results would indicate that while criminal justice involvement may ultimately result in exposure of the child victim to the full impact of an adversary judicial system, such exposure is in fact rare and not necessarily excessively traumatic in nature. Parenthetically, these findings are somewhat depressing in terms of the relative infrequency with which prosecutorial actions result in offender conviction.

Child victims seen by CPC-SU (based on 1978 and 1979 cases) range in age from 6 months through 17 and one-half years, with a mean age of 8 years and 8 months. Twenty-nine percent of these children are boys. Slightly over 60 percent of these cases involve what we consider a more serious form of sexual abuse (i.e., vaginal or anal intercourse; oral sodomy). Forty-seven percent involve multiple offenses over time. Alleged offenders are almost invariably male (97%); forty-one percent are members of the child's immediate or extended family (23% are parents or parent surrogates).

Of 261 police cases tracked through the criminal justice system, 223 (85%) were forwarded to prosecutors; the remainder were either considered unfounded cases (N = 8) or cases with continuing investigation (N = 25) or cases closed through arrest on a different charge (N = 5). Ninety-six of the forwarded cases (43%) involved adult suspects; the remainder were cases with juvenile offenders.

Of the 223 cases forwarded for prosecution, four percent (N = 7 adult and 3 juvenile) were dropped because the family (i.e., parents) refused to press charges; most of these were cases involving extended family members as the abusers. Thirty-three percent (N = 32 adult and 41 juvenile) exited from the system because the arrest warrant or custody order (juvenile offenders) applications were denied by prosecutors. An offender was arrested in 63% of the cases forwarded for prosecution (N = 57 adult and 83 juvenile). In over fifty percent of those cases where a warrant or custody order application was denied the stated reason was lack of corroborative evidence. The second most common reason for prosecutors denying arrest applications was a lack of consistency in the victim's story over time (12%).

Twelve percent (N = 3 adult and 14 juvenile) of all cases where an arrest was made (N = 140) were "no papered" (i.e., not formally charged). An additional eleven percent (N = 15 adult) of these cases were not indicted by the grand jury. At the time of this analysis, three cases were still awaiting a grand jury hearing, and nineteen (9 adult and 10 juvenile) were awaiting trial; eighty-five cases (N = 26 adult and 59 juvenile) had "gone to court."

Twenty-eight percent (N = 2 adult and 22 juvenile) of those cases going to court were dismissed, usually at the request of prosecution. Sixty-two percent of all cases going to court resulted in a guilty plea (N = 21 adult and 32 juvenile, including 5 consent decrees). A total of eight cases (9%; N = 3 adult and 5 juvenile) actually went to trial; of these, all but one (an adult offender) resulted in a conviction. Based upon the results presented above, if you are a victim of sexual abuse whose case has been forwarded for prosecution in the District of Columbia, the odds are:

—two to one that the offender will be arrested
—slightly less than one in three that the offender will be convicted
—less than one in eight that you will have to face a grand jury
—less than one in twenty that you will have to testify at trial
—less than two in one hundred that you will have to testify in open (i.e., adult) criminal trial

These findings, although somewhat discouraging regarding likelihood of conviction, are encouraging in other respects. They clearly suggest that having to face the potential trauma of having to testify in open court and undergo cross-examination is the rare exception rather than the rule. Second, the conviction rates themselves, although substantially less than the two-thirds of all felony arrests resulting in conviction in the District of Columbia in 1978 (Joint Committee on Judicial Administration in the District of Columbia, Note 2), are substantially higher than the 22% of arrests leading to conviction for sexual offenses against children (excluding exhibitionism) in the District of Columbia from 1971 to 1975 reported by Williams (Note 3).

In addition to the data presented on processing of adult and juvenile criminal proceedings, data are recorded on forty-four cases forwarded for family court action under the District of Columbia's Prevention of Child Abuse and Neglect Act (these were primarily cases involving parent or caretaker abusers). Of these forty-four cases, 10 (23%) were not petitioned (i.e., "no papered") by prosecutors. Of the thirty-four petitioned cases, six(18%) were dismissed. At the time of analyses, five cases were still awaiting court action. The remaining 23 cases were all resolved through parental stipulation of the facts rather than an adversary hearing. Two-thirds of these cases (i.e., those resolved) resulted in the placement of the child in foster care with the remaining one-third remaining in the home under protective supervision.

Discussion

The findings presented here would suggest that, at least in regard to District of Columbia cases, concerns expressed by others regarding the impact of adversarial court proceedings on child victims are somewhat misplaced primarily because so few children actually have to testify in court. Of those that must testify, most testify in juvenile court without the publicity attendant with an adult criminal proceeding.

That a relatively large proportion of forwarded complaints are dropped due to lack of corroboration is not particularly surprising in that the District of Columbia, through judicial precedent, remains one of the few jurisdictions in the U.S. which maintains a special corroboration requirement for minor (i.e., juvenile) complainants in rape and other sexual victimization cases. It is interesting to note that while other federal courts have held that no special corroboration requirement is necessary with minor complainants (e.g., *United States v. Bear Runner*, 1978), the District of Columbia Court of Appeals (part of the federal court system) has ruled otherwise. Currently, 29 states have abolished the corroboration requirement in all sexual assault cases, while four retain it for all child victims; the remaining states impose corroboration requirements under special circumstances (Davidson and Bulkley, 1980). Although Leahy (1979) has urged the retention of a special corroboration requirement in intrafamily cases, in general it appears that the trend of the last decade is to remove this special condition from child complainant cases as it has already been removed from adult complaint (i.e., adult rape) cases.

The remaining jurisdictions still requiring special corroboration of the child victim's complaint highlight the somewhat schizoid view of child victims generally held by the legal community. On the one hand, special procedures or protections for the child victim in the court process are resisted on the grounds that child victims of sexual offenses do not constitute a special class apart from other victims. On the other hand, many jurisdictions impose specific procedural barriers to treatment of the child victim as if he or she were an adult. In addition to special corroboration requirements, these barriers include; the use of lie detectors and psychiatric examinations as means of assessing complainant credibility in some jurisdictions (Legrand & Chappell, Note 4); permitting introduction of the defense that the child victim was of "unchaste" character in at least six states (although prior victim sexual behavior is no longer considered pertinent for adult victims except to the extent it sheds light on the issue of consent with a particular defendant; Children's Rights Report, Note 5); and, the almost universal prosecutorial practice of declining complaints initiated by minors unless the minor's parents are also in favor of prosecution (or the alleged offender is the parent).

Although our experience is that few child victims actually end up having to testify in court, it is true that for those who do the experience can be traumatic—we have also found, however, that the court proceeding can have beneficial outcomes for the child. Children, like adults, often have strong feelings regarding their victimization and want the offender to be punished for his wrongdoing. Court proceedings are the only way that the victim can legally seek retribution against the perpetrator. Older children in particular often have a strong sense of social responsibility and will choose to proceed with prosecution even though it may be stressful in the belief that they are helping to protect other children from being victimized. In many instances, court proceedings also serve to enhance the child's sense of personal vindication—others are treating the child's victimization as a serious matter; are tangibly expressing their trust and faith in the child's story. Bohmer (1974) in a survey of judicial opinions found that while 84% of judges responding felt that it was traumatic for child rape victims to testify, fully one-half of these judges also believed that procedural changes could be made to help reduce this trauma. Specific recommendations included private hearings, greater reliance on depositions, and clearing the courtroom of all but involved parties. Currently, three states (Arizona, New Mexico, and Montana) allow videotaping of the child victim's testimony (including cross-examination) with the defendant and his attorney present for later replaying in the court and at least two other states (Minnesota and Massachusetts) allow exclusion of the public in child sexual assault cases. Similar procedures, if adopted elsewhere would substantially reduce the possibly traumatic impact of the courtroom proceeding on these children.

Finally, two additional constitutionally acceptable modifications of the court process could substantially reduce the portential for trauma to child victims participating in the court process. First, it should be established as routine procedure that either the parents of child victims, or other supportive persons of the child's choice be allowed as a matter of course to be present in juvenile court proceedings when the child must testify. It is somewhat ironic that the juvenile court in the interest of minimizing the deleterious impact of its proceedings on the juvenile offender often enhances the stress placed on the child victim by barring all but witnesses from the proceeding.

Second, there appear to be no constitutional barriers to greater reliance upon hearsay evidence rather than actual testimony at stages prior to trial. In the District of Columbia, hearsay evidence is routinely allowed in these cases in lieu of testimony at the preliminary hearing but not in the Grand Jury proceeding. In some jurisdictions the child victim is routinely expected to testify at all three proceedings (i.e., preliminary hearing, grand jury, and trial). Acceptance of hearsay evidence in place of formal testimony for all stages prior to actual trial would further limit the number of times a child victim is required to give formal testimony. In addition, given the propensity for cases to either be dismissed or resolved through pleas, use of hearsay evidence might totally obviate the need for the vast majority of child victims to publicly and formally testify.

Well-intentioned yet misguided concerns for the safety and well-being of child victims of sexual assault have led many to conclude that initiation of court proceedings in cases of child sexual victimization pose too great a risk of psychological trauma for the child victim. The alternative view, presented here and elsewhere (e.g., Conte & Berliner, in press) is that these risks have been over-stated, and that in any event there exist practical and effective procedures which, if adopted, will minimize the likelihood that any child will be harmed by the court experience. Our goal should not be to retreat from involvement with the prosecutorial systems but rather to exert our efforts and influence to make law enforcement and judicial systems responsive to the needs of these children. To do otherwise is to both deny the legitimate demands of many victimized children for justice, and to tacitly decriminalize acts of molestation, sodomy, and rape when perpetrated upon children.

REFERENCE NOTES

1. Bach, C. & Anderson, S. Adolescent sexual abuse and assault. Paper presented at the Second International Congress on Adolescent Medicine, May, 1979.
2. Joint Committee on Judicial Administration in the District of Columbia and the Executive Officer. *1978 Annual Report.* Washington, D.C.: District of Columbia Courts, 1978.
3. Williams, K. *The prosecution of sexual assaults* (pamphlet). Washington, D.C.: Institute for Law and Social Research, 1978.
4. Legrand, C. & Chappell, D. *Forcible rape: An analysis of legal issues.* Report prepared for the National Institute of Law Enforcement and Criminal Justice, Dept. of Justice by the Battelle Law and Justice Study Center.
5. *Children's Rights Reports,* 1978, *11*(6). Newsletter published by the Juvenile Rights Project of the American Civil Liberties Union, N.Y., N.Y.

REFERENCES

Child victims of incest. Denver: American Humane Association, 1968.
Benward, J. & Densen-Gerber, J. Incest as a causative factor in antisocial behavior; An exploratory study. *Contemporary Drug Problems,* 1975, 4(3) 323–340.
Bohmer, C. Judicial attitudes toward rape victims. *Judicature,* 1974, *57*(7), 303–307.
Burgess, A. & Holstrom, L. The child and family during the court process. In A. Burgess, A. Groth, L. Holstrom, & S. Sgroi, *Sexual assault of children and adolescents.* Lexington, Mass.: Heath & Co., 1978.
Davidson, H. & Bulkley, J. *Child sexual abuse: Legal issues and approaches.* Washington, D.C.: American Bar Assoc., 1980.
Conte, J. & Berliner, L. Prosecution of the offender in cases of sexual assault against children. *Victimology,*(in press).
Finkelhor, D. *Sexually victimized children.* New York.: MacMillan, 1979.
Forward, S. & Buck, C. *Betrayal of innocence: Incest and its devastation.* New York.: Penguin Books, 1978.
Gagnon, J. Female child victims of sex offenses. *Social Problems,* 1965, *13*, 176–192.
Greenberg, N. The epidemiology of childhood sexual abuse. *Pediatric Annals,* 1979, 8(5), 16–28.
Halleck, S. The physician's role in the management of victims of sexual offenders. *Journal of American Medical Association,* 1962, *180*, 273–278.
James, J. & Meyerding, J. Early sexual experience as a factor in prostitution. *Archives of Sexual Behavior,* 1977, 7(1), 31–42.
Kirkwood, L. Mahaila, M. Incest and the legal system: Inadequacies and alternatives. *University of California at Davis Law Review,* 1979, *12*(2), 673–679.
Landis, J. Experience of 500 children with adult sexual deviates. *Psychiatric Quality Supplements,* 1956, *30*, 91–109.
Libai, D. The protection of the child victim of a sexual offense in the criminal justice system. *Wayne Law Review,* 1969, *15*, 979–986.

Leahy, M. United States v. Bear Runner: The need for corroboration in incest cases. *St Louis University Law Journal,* 1979, *23*(4), 747–767.

Peters, J. Children who are victims of sexual assault and the psychology of offenders. *American Journal of Psychotherapy,* 1976, *30,* 378–421.

Stevens, D. & Berliner, L. Special techniques for child witnesses. In L. Schultz (ed.), *The sexual victimology of youth.* Springfield, Ill.: C.C. Thomas, 1980.

Summit, R. & Kryso, J. Sexual abuse of children: A clinical spectrum. *American Journal of Orthopsychiatry,* 1978, *48,* 237–251.

United States v. Bear Runner, 547F.2D 966 (8th Cir., 1978).

MANAGEMENT AND TREATMENT OF CHILD SEXUAL ABUSE CASES IN A JUVENILE COURT SETTING

Joseph Zefran Jr., MSW
Harry F. Riley, MSW
William O. Andersen, MA
Jeanne H. Curtis, MEd
Linda M. Jackson, MSW
Paul H. Kelly, MA
Ellen T. McGury, MA
Mary K. Suriano, MSW

The number of child sexual abuse treatment programs has been increasing in the past few years. The Juvenile Court of Cook County, the oldest Juvenile Court in the country (established in 1899), became a part of this trend with the establishment of its program, the Special Services Unit for the Treatment of Child Sexual Abuse. This article provides a discussion of the case management, legal, and therapeutic issues involved in the handling of child sexual abuse cases at a juvenile court. The article is based, in part, on data describing the experiences gained in providing service to a sample (N = 55 families) of sexually abusing families referred to the Court's Special Services Unit during the first nine months of 1980. In the 55 families, 72 children were victims of sexual abuse. There were a total of 59 abusers of whom 33% were natural fathers, 48% parenting figure (e.g., stepfathers, foster father, mother's paramour), and 19% other relatives. The average age of the child victim is 10 with 96% of victims being female. Thirty-nine percent are Caucasian, 51% Black, and 10% other.

Clinical Characteristics

Qualitative descriptions of the clinical characteristics of the families and individuals involved in the sexual abuse were synthesized from the records of the Unit's Probation Officers.*

Family Characteristics

All of the sexually abusive families referred to the Unit were described as being dysfunctional; families differed only in the degree and type of dysfunction. They were characterized by a lack of productive communication, and as lacking in generational boundaries (that is, parents play the role of child and child plays the role of parent). Parents often sought to receive nurturance from their children rather than to provide it for them. Parents would abdicate their decision-making responsibility, leaving children to provide their own structure. Families were also described as exhibiting extremes in their emotional expression; affect was either very flat or was expressed in continual verbal conflict and physical violence. Power between the parents was unequal; one parent, usually the father-figure, was over-bearing, while the other was weak. As a consequence, the children's behavior was either under-structured (few controls) or over-structured (rigid, irrational demands). The families showed little or no problem-solving ability and were largely unable to produce or pursue satisfactory alternatives to internal or external stresses. Finally, nearly all of the sexually abusive families were characterized by social isolation. Positive or negative relationships with people and institutions outside the family were severely restricted to those contacts necessary (work, school, etc.) to maintain subsistence and isolation.

Child Victim Characteristics

The clinical description of the child victims of sexual abuse yielded several common characteristics. Victims were described as experiencing depression, guilt, anger, low self-esteem, and a lack of ability to trust. The victims were described as exhibiting these un-

---

*Because this article was written by employees of the Juvenile Court of Cook County, the term "probation officer" is used. This term applies to all professionals, in court or non-court settings, who specialize in therapeutic services.

derlying traits through two different sets of behaviors—active or passive. The *active* victims were those who ran away from home, who abused drugs or alcohol, who engaged in promiscuous sexual activity, or who attempted suicide. They were often highly verbal in treatment sessions to the point of being overeager to disclose all the details of the sexual abuse, even in the first meeting with the Unit's Probation Officer. They often displayed a pseudo-sophistication, appearing to be older than their chronological age. The *passive* victims, on the other hand, were described as being withdrawn, fearful, and showing little or no affect. They maintained few, if any, social contacts with their peers. In appearance and attitude, they exhibited an aversion to their sexuality; some were obese, some were unconcerned about their personal hygiene. Many engaged in infantile behaviors. Although extremely non-verbal in the initial stages of treatment, the *passive* victims usually developed trust in the therapist and arrived at a genuine awareness of their feelings sooner in the treatment process than did the *active* victims.

Abuser Characteristics

All the abusers referred to the Unit were males who were described as having low self-esteem, poor impulse control, a high degree of guilt, and an inability to trust or experience intimacy in relationships. It was also reported that few of the abusers ever had a satisfying relationship with an adult female. (Besides these common characteristics, the clinical descriptions of the abusers by the Unit's Probation Officers closely paralleled the categorization of abusers defined by Blair and Rita Justicè—symbiotic (introvert, rationalizer, tyrant, and alcoholic), psychopathic, pedophiliac, and psychotic (Justice and Justice, 1970.)

Mother Characteristics

The clinical descriptions of the non-abusing mothers can be categorized into five types: *passive, dominant, absent, disabled,* and *nurturing.* The majority of mothers were described as weak, unassertive, and overdependent. Chronic depression, low self-esteem, and a sense of being overwhelmed also characterized *passive* mothers. Many would engage in role reversal with their daughters; the daughter would be expected to assume adult roles of providing nurturance and assuming responsibility for decision-making, household chores, and act as a sexual partner to the spouse. Some mothers were themselves victimized as battered women. In contrast, the few *dominant* mothers seen by the Unit were described as having the power in the family, as being intimidating to the abuser and others, as accusing the child victim of lying about the sexual abuse, and as stubbornly denying to outsiders that the abuse occurred. A few were *absent* mothers who would not or could not be part of the family due to physical, emotional, or mental disability, or who simply stayed away from the home for varying periods of time. The second most frequent type of non-abusing mothers were *nurturing* toward their children. These mothers were able and willing to provide support and protection for their children and were able to make decisions about their future relationships with their spouses and about other important issues.

Therapeutic, Case Management, and Legal Roles

As required by Illinois law, all reports of child abuse and neglect are made to the Illinois Department of Children and Family Services (IDCFS). For cases first reported to the police or the courts, IDCFS must also be notified regardless of whether or not the police or the courts continue their involvement. In Cook County, approximately 10% of reported child sexual abuse cases are referred to the Juvenile Court by IDCFS officials. Most cases are referred to a purchase-of-service agency whose focus is to work with intact families and to avoid court involvement. Thus, cases generally referred to Juvenile Court have been pre-screened to include the severely dysfunctional families whose children need involuntary placement and to exclude the mildly dysfunctional families who voluntarily agree to treatment and are more likely to remain or be reunited as a family unit. With such families, the Unit's Probation Officer fulfills the role of a clinical social worker while the IDCFS Child Protective Service (CPS) worker fulfills the role of a case manager.

The major role of the probation officer is that of a catalyst, one who offers help and support for the client so that positive change in behavior and psychological growth and development can occur. The role of the case manager who functions in a child protective service capacity involves investigation, case planning, and service procurement. The roles of prosecuting attorneys, defense attorneys, Guardian ad Litem attorneys, and judges are, in part, determined by the adversarial nature of juvenile courts. Under a set of rather precise legal rules, the attorneys must present formal evidence regarding the allegations. The judge must weigh the evidence and decide the truth of the allegations and make a legal disposition.

Each of the three groups of professionals in Juvenile Court have specific roles in the handling of the Juvenile Court's cases involving child sexual abuse. The IDCFS/CPS case managers are responsible for: (1) the initial investigation, case plan, and recommendations; (2) the referral of the case to the court; (3) periodic reports to court on the overall progress of the case as well as violations of court orders; (4) arrangements for out-of-home placement when necessary; and (5) the referral of clients for necessary services. The Unit's Probation Officers are responsible for: (1) the assessment of the degree of psychological trauma suffered by family members as a result of the sexual abuse; (2) the assessment of the strengths, dysfunction, and motivation of the family; (3) the plan of treatment intervention; (4) building therapeutic relationships and engaging clients in treatment; and (5) to provide treatment to clients in order to achieve the Unit's major goals of ensuring to the child victim protection from further abuse and of alleviating the trauma of the sexual abuse so that the victim and other family members are able to grow as "mature persons" (Satir, 1967, p. 91).

The specific roles of the Juvenile Court's legal professionals are defined by the Court's judicial process goals, which are to: (1) provide for the protection of child victims of sexual abuse from any future sexual or physical abuse either by allowing the family to remain together (only after the safety of the child has been assured), or by removal of the abuser from the home, or by removal of the child; (2) make certain that the child victims of sexual abuse and their families receive immediate therapeutic services to ameliorate the especially negative impact of sexual abuse on their proper development; (3) handle the prosecution of sexually abusive family members so that not only will the protection of the child victims be provided for, but also that the family ties be preserved and strengthened; (4) secure for the child victim, whose removal from the home is deemed necessary, those out-of-home placements that will provide, in accordance with the Juvenile Court Act, such care and guidance as will serve the moral, emotional, mental and physical welfare of the child; and (5) promptly ascertain all jurisdictional facts relative to the current condition and future welfare of the child in a manner that recognizes the uniqueness of the trauma suffered by child victims of sexual abuse.

In keeping with these goals, the specific roles of the judge are to: (1) preside over the presentation of facts alleging the sexual abuse; (2) to decide the truth of the allegations; and (3) to enter interim or dispositional orders for the protection of the child in keeping with the best interests of family members. The roles of the Assistant State's Attorneys (prosecutors) are to: (1) bring together the legal facts of proof of the allegations of sexual abuse through interviews with those involved; (2) present those facts in court; (3) request orders of protection when necessary; and (4) prepare the child victim for testimony in court when such testimony is essential. The role of the Public Defender or privately-retained defense attorney is to defend the rights of the abusing parent(s) either by presenting facts in court which contradict the allegations of sexual abuse or by presenting the mitigating circumstances which led to the abuse. In cases where the parent was not the alleged abuser but is accused of failure to prevent the sexual abuse, the role of the defense attorneys in defending the rights of the parent remains. The role of the Guardian ad Litem is to ensure that the rights and best interests of the child victim are assured. This is necessary because the victim's best interests may be of secondary importance to prosecuting and defense attorneys whose roles are mandated to exclude primary focus on the rights of the child.

Coordination Between Therapeutic and Case Management Professionals

The role of a probation officer specializing in therapeutic services is a relatively new concept in juvenile justice and may result in some confusion on the part of clients and other professionals about this role. The IDCFS/CPS case manager who is handling the referral to Juvenile Court of a child sexual abuse case for the first time, for example, is likely to be unaware of the treatment role of the Unit's Probation Officer. The CPS worker may assume that the role of the Unit's Probation Officer is like the role traditionally performed by a Probation Officer (that is, making reports to the Court, providing casework counseling, and procuring other services needed by the client). Even when the CPS case manager and the Unit's Probation

Officer have had a clear understanding of their respective roles, the communication of these roles to clients may be difficult when clients are in a crisis state. There are, however, several ways to minimize these problems:

First, the administrators of the Juvenile Court and IDCFS agreed that, since IDCFS had the legal responsibility to do the investigation, planning, and case management, the IDCFS workers would fulfill that role by submitting the social investigation and progress reports and by giving testimony required in the legal proceedings. Since IDCFS is the primary child welfare agency in Illinois with greater access to services and placement facilities, the IDCFS case manager makes all arrangements for those services and placement facilities needed by the clients. The Probation Officers of the Court's Special Services Unit would be responsible only for the treatment of the clients and for submitting reports on the clinical aspects of the case. This interagency agreement has reduced disagreement and confusion among staff within the two agencies.

Second, the agreed upon roles of the IDCFS case manager and the Unit's Probation Officers in regard to court hearings were communicated to the attorneys and judges at Juvenile Court assigned to specialize in child sexual abuse cases. In periodic meetings between the legal professionals and the Unit, it was agreed that the Unit's Probation Officers would never be called to testify as witnesses in trial proceedings, but would only be requested to amplify written reports as to the progress of treatment or to be present in court as an advocate for the family. This understanding was essential in order to avoid damaging the trusting, supportive relationships between the Unit's Probation Officer and the clients.

Third, beginning at the time of referral to the Unit, the IDCFS case manager and the Unit's Probation Officers would regularly meet not only to clarify roles, but also to discuss the overall features of the case plan and to decide on the performance of specific tasks. An example of this might involve the case of a child victim who is currently placed in a foster home, but who is ready to be returned home with her non-abusing mother. Although the interagency agreement specified that the IDCFS case manager would arrange for placement, it may be decided at the case staffing that the task of discussing the change in placement with the child and the mother would best be handled by the Unit's Probation Officer; the task of the actual move would then be handled by the IDCFS worker.

Fourth, shortly after a case is referred to the Unit, the Unit's Probation Officer and the IDCFS case manager would meet together with the clients to clarify for the clients what each professional will do.

Coordination Between Therapeutic and Legal Professionals

Just as role confusion may create problems between case managers and probation officers, role conflict may create coordination problems between legal professionals and probation officers, especially with regard to child sexual abuse cases. Conflicts may occur between the two groups because of the contrast in roles and communication styles arising from the difference in attitudes and educational backgrounds. Probation officers are trained in understanding individual and family psychodynamics and in the use of treatment techniques to improve human functioning. By contrast, legal professionals are trained in understanding the logic of law and in the use of evidence and motions to prove their side of a case. Attitudinally, probation officers tend to be supportive, flexible, and accepting; legal professionals tend to be logical, precise, and adversarial. These two groups of professionals also use a different terminology and language which can create communication problems. Therapeutic specialists who are unaccustomed to working with legal professionals in a court setting may not appreciate the importance of legal issues such as the rights of due process, rules of evidence, and dispositional orders. Conversely, attorneys and judges who handle child sexual abuse cases may not appreciate the importance of clinical issues such as family dysfunction, nurturance, and impulse control. The differences in roles and communication styles may cause these two groups of professionals to avoid attempts to respect and appreciate the roles and viewpoints of each other. A lack of mutual respect increases the possibility that tragic consequences may occur for family members involved in child sexual abuse. For example, a child victim may be further victimized if the probation officers, attorneys, and the judge fail to cooperate in synthesizing information required for a protective order. The non-court therapeutic specialist, lacking appreciation of the legal requirements of rules of evidence, may fail to communicate observations in a way that would enable the legal professionals to legally justify the protective order. Conversely, the legal professional, lacking appreciation for the probation officer's expert assessment of the severity of individual and family dysfunction, may fail to communicate his/her observations of the legal aspects in a way that would enable the probation officer to cooperate in obtaining a protective order. However, when there exists an atmosphere of respect and cooperation between probation officers and legal professionals, several benefits are possible.

First, the child victim of sexual abuse is assured that he or she is believed beyond a reasonable doubt. Through the power of the court, the child is further assured that he or she will be reasonably protected from further abuse and will receive treatment necessary to help minimize whatever trauma was suffered as a result of the abuse. Second, the abuser benefits when the probation officers and the legal professionals cooperate to elicit admission of the sexual abuse. Clinically, the abuser becomes free to redirect the energy spent in denying the abuse toward involving himself/herself in treatment which is necessary for reintegration of self toward normal growth and development. The abuser may also avoid being sent to jail and be allowed to receive the treatment which often helps the abuser remain with the family, not as an abuser, but as a nurturing and nurtured parent and spouse. For example, of the 59 abusers referred to the Unit during the first nine months of 1980, only 18 were involved in criminal court proceedings. Of the 18, 4 cases were pending at the close of the study. Of the remaining 14 cases, only 3 resulted in jail sentences, 7 resulted in probation or supervision with treatment, and 4 were dismissed. Conte and Berliner (In press) report similar findings with a sample of cases in the Seattle program. Contrary to popular belief, the justice system rarely acts in a strictly punitive way toward child sexual abusers.

Having discussed the management issues, the following section describes the treatment methods developed by the Unit's Probation Officers.

Treatment Methods

Families involved in child sexual abuse can be categorized into three types. The first is the *family-without-abuser* situation where the non-abusing parent (usually the mother), the victim, and other siblings are reunited or remain together after the abuser (usually the father) has permanently left the home. The second category is the *family-together* situation in which the family will either remain together or will eventually be reunited as a whole family. This type is the one most frequently described in the literature (Giarretto, 1976; Meiselman, 1979; Muldoon, 1979). The third category is the *victim-without-family* situation in which the victim is likely to remain permanently in placement outside the home due to the inability or unwillingness of the parents to work toward the child's return. Of the 55 families described at the beginning of this article, 29% (16) fell into the *family-without-abuser* category, 15% (8) into the *family-together* category, and 49% (27) into the *victim-without-family* category. It was also found that the duration of treatment for all three categories of cases is from one to three years, with most cases in treatment for two years.

Family-Without-Abuser Treatment

In the *family-without-abuser* category, the primary clients are the non-abusing mother and the victim. The abuser has agreed to leave the home permanently or has been ordered to do so by the spouse. Thus, the abuser is not available for treatment nor, in many cases, for court involvement. There are three strategies of intervention with this category.

First, and most critical, is the work done with the victim to minimize the trauma of the abuse. The first step is to help the victim to verbalize feelings by creating an atmosphere of caring and support through responses and body language which convey acceptance. Emphasis should be placed on the fact that the victim is not the only child to have experienced sexual abuse. After sufficient trust has been established in individual treatment, placing the child in group therapy with other sexually abused victims may be considered. Group therapy techniques which focus on a sharing of experiences are very helpful in reducing the victim's sense of isolation and in building a network of supportive relationships. After passing through the initial state of crisis reaction, victims often begin exhibiting internal and external destructive behavior patterns, resulting from being more in touch with their anger at being abused. Some victims may be verbally hostile or may act out sexually; others become depressed, reclusive, or even suicidal. To counteract these destructive behaviors, the victim's constructive behavior patterns should be emphasized and reinforced while also helping the victim to appropriately focus previously repressed, angry feelings toward the abuser or other family members.

Second, treatment must also focus on the non-abusing mother. Although these mothers often have low self-esteem and little knowledge or confidence in parenting skills, they are often motivated toward placing the needs of their children over their need to remain with the abusing spouses. Their strong needs for affection and intimacy are not unlike those of an adolescent. Thus, they may also seek a role reversal with their children (usually daughters). This is compounded by the absence of the spouse which often means decreased financial resources. Thus, concrete casework services may be needed to apply for financial assistance, to locate new housing, or to find employment. Success in such activities can be very therapeutic in building self-esteem and a greater sense of independence. After the mother's crisis reactions have subsided, group therapy for single-parent mothers of sexually abused children may be useful in reducing the mother's own sense of guilt and isolation. Community activity groups may be helpful in building a new support network and in mobilizing the mother to overcome depression.

The third phase of treatment with the *family-without-abuser* case should focus on the relationship between the mother and her child victim. The first step in rebuilding that relationship is similar to the first step in individual treatment of the child and the mother; that is, they need to express their individual feelings about the sexual abuse to each other. Following this, the mother and daughter can be helped to resolve their feelings about the sexual abuse in the context of their relationship. An example of this might be a case in which a mother was told of the abuse by her daughter but failed to stop it. The mother may need to explain to her daughter why she could not protect her or she may need to apologize to her daughter for her failure. The mother is then able to express feelings of love and caring toward her daughter. The daughter, after expressing anger at the mother for failing to stop the sexual abuse, would reiterate her own feelings of love and caring. After the mother and daughter have mutually shared and responded to each other's feeling about the sexual abuse, treatment can proceed into the next phase of the rebuilding of the mother-daughter relationship as one based on mutual trust and caring. This involves the clarification of needs - the need of the victim for support and affection and guidance, the need of the mother for affection and respect as a parent. This process also allows mother and daughter to reduce their isolation and re-establish generational boundaries.

Family-Together Treatment

The treatment of the *family-together* type of case follows closely that process described most frequently in existing literature (Giarretto, 1976; Meiselman, 1979; and Muldoon, 1979). The victim will be interviewed first and seen in individual therapy throughout the process. Mother-victim sessions will follow to strengthen that relationship and allow the victim to release anger and allow the mother to show her support. If mother does not totally believe her child, these sessions can enable the mother to clarify her doubts. Because of the presence of the probation officer with whom the victim has a trusting relationship, the victim often feels safe to discuss the abuse with the mother and the mother is helped to realize and believe that the abuse did occur. The most important outcome of the mother-victim treatment phase is that the mother clearly communicate to her child that she believes the victim and will protect the victim in the future.

The treatment of the abuser, usually the father or father-substitute, is a crucial part of working with *family-together* cases. Because it is rare that the abuser admits to the sexual abuse and because any treatment must begin with an acknowledgement and acceptance of the problem, the primary treatment objective in the first few individual sessions is to enable the abuser to admit that he has sexually abused the child. At the same time, he is being alerted to the possible consequences of his denial or of his admission to the abuse. The use of court sanctions (e.g., jail time) can be helpful in this process. The fear of punishment may motivate the abuser, albeit reluctantly, to make an admission at least on a cognitive level (e.g., he reasons that such an admission will keep him out of jail). However, the kind of admission necessary for treatment must be made not only on the basis of "reason" but must also involve the abuser's acceptance of his feelings of guilt, anger, fear, and the need to protect himself. Court ordered treatment can provide the abuser with the opportunity for treatment where he can more safely experience these feelings and be free to make a full admission to himself and to the probation officer. When he is able to fully admit to the abuse and to realize that he can be helped and get his family back together, he begins treatment with the child and with the spouse/ partner; he may also continue with individual sessions. In sessions with the child, he can free himself of immobilizing guilt by admitting to, apologizing for, and taking full responsibility for the sexual abuse. Also as important is his promise to the child that he will not abuse again. The treatment can then evolve into re-establishing the generational boundaries and trust levels necessary to strengthening their relationship. Work can also begin with the abuser in discovering why the abuse began and what changes are necessary to prevent it in the future. This often means that the couple begin marital or couples counseling.

The experience of the Unit's Probation Officers is that the final phase of family therapy can begin *only after* individual treatment with the victim, abuser, and non-abusing parent and after treatment with the victim-parent, abuser-spouse, victim-abuser dyads. In the family systems approach used by the Unit's Probation Officers, it is believed that the family cannot function as a growth-producing system if members of that system are dysfunctional. When family therapy is attempted before the feelings and issues have been resolved in individual and dyad treatment, the Unit's Probation Officers have found that family therapy is not successful and, in some cases, is detrimental to further treatment. The approximate sequence of individual-dyad-family treatment should *always* be followed.

In treating the family as a whole, emphasis is placed on the effect each member has on the total system; that is, on the relationships among members, on the flexibility of boundaries in the family, and on the ability of the system to contribute to and accept from sources outside the family. When the abuser or victim is living out of the home, family therapy should begin *before* reunification and then continue for some period afterwards. If the family has remained together, family therapy can only begin *after* the trauma of the abuse has been resolved in individual or dyad sessions or in victims and parents groups. Behaviors which signal the resolution of trauma include the cessation of all sexually abusive behavior; the child victim's establishment of traditional peer group friendships; the parents resumption of their role as parents (nurturing and limit-setting activity); the parents' allowing their children to act as children in age-appropriate ways; the parents' achievement of a satifying relationship, including resumption of a satisfying sexual relationship; the ability of the family to create alternatives in solving problems; and the recognition of their needs and the ability to seek need fulfillment.

Victim-Without-Family Treatment

Techniques useful with clients in this final category include a combination of those used with child victims in the two categories discussed above and those which are used with children in permanent or semi-permanent foster care. In these cases where reunification of child with family is not likely, the parents have allowed the care of their child to be assumed by the courts and placement agencies rather than risk further involvement by outsiders either in terms of court proceedings or in terms of therapeutic intervention. In some instances, the victim's mother is highly dependent upon her spouse or partner and consequently sees no choice but to remain with them even though it means separation from her child. In other cases, the mother may be a battered wife unable to protect even herself. Physical or mental disability may also make care of the child impossible. In this type of fragmented "family," there is only one identified client—the victim. There are three important issues in the treatment of child victims in the *victim-without-family* situation. First, the goals of the initial phase of treatment dealing with the effects of the sexual abuse are similar to the treatment goals with victims of the other two categories - reduction of trauma, fear, isolation, guilt, and depression. Because there are no parents to interact with, there is often greater difficulty in helping this type of victim place the responsibility for the sexual abuse on the abuser rather than on herself or himself. The amount of anger may be greater too because there are two causes for it—the sexual abuse and the parental rejection. The fact that this kind of child victim has suffered such a basic loss makes it all the more necessary that the probation officer firmly establish a supportive, trusting relationship.

Second, after some resolution of the effects of the abuse, it is equally important that treatment be focused on the reality of the child's situation; the strong possibility that the child will not return home. The probation officer and the child should openly and jointly explore the idea of permanency planning. Issues of adjustment to the new living arrangement need to be dealt with—change in schools, change in neighborhood environment, and changes involved in relationships to the child's new "family" members.

Finally, it has been found that children in the *victim-without-family* situation often have a greater need to reduce their isolation than those who still have one or both parents available to them. Therefore, it is extremely important that consideration be given to placing the child in a victims' group, especially one of longer duration (i.e., approximately six months).

The Unit's experience with victims' groups indicate that groups are more successful when potential group members are matched on the basis of similarity of age, psychological development, and nature of issues they need to work on. For instance, a group of victims who need only to work on the effects of the sexual abuse ordinarily should not be grouped with those who have other important issues, such as the effects of permanent placement out of the home.

Summary

The principle factor in the Juvenile Court's approach to the management and treatment of child sexual abuse is to assure the protection of the child victim from further abuse. Protection of the child is primary because it is the mandate given to the Juvenile Court and because it is the necessary first step in the treatment process. The management and treatment of child sexual abuse is a highly complex problem requiring the intervention and cooperation of professionals from different fields of expertise. In one sense, the complex nature of child sexual abuse requires the most skilled and sophisticated treatment techniques available. Yet, in another sense, the treatment of child sexual abuse also requires something so simple and basic that, without it, success in treatment is nearly impossible. The members of the Special Services Unit have found that the most important factor in the successful treatment of the child victims of sexual abuse is the genuine caring of the therapist. The child victim has been forced to undergo what is perhaps the most damaging experience a child can have—the violation and betrayal of the trust and caring between parent and child. As one child victim put it, "sexual abuse is when your dad doesn't really love you and just pretends to . . . what hurts is when your dad is just using you" (Armstrong, 1978, p. 133). It is precisely because of this that consistent caring by the therapist-adult figure is essential to successful treatment. Child sexual abuse victims are highly sensitive to any nuance of insincerity. In the words of a Probation Officer in the Juvenile Court's Special

Services Unit, "The only way I found to convey the feeling of caring is to really feel it!"

REFERENCES

Armstrong, L. *Kiss Daddy Goodnight.* New York, New York: Hawthorn Books, 1978.

Conte, J.R. and Berliner, Lucy. Prosecution of the offender in cases of sexual assault against children. *Victimology,* (In Press).

Giarretto, H. The treatment of father-daughter incest: A psychosocial approach. *Children Today.* July-August, 1976, 5(4), 2–6.

Justice, B. and Justice, R. *The Broken Taboo.* New York: Human Sciences Press, 1979.

Meiselman, K.C. *Incest: A Psychological Study of Causes and Effects.* San Francisco: Jossey-Bass Publishers, 1978.

Muldoon, L. *Incest: Confronting the silent crime.* St. Paul, Minnesota: The Minnesota Program for Victims of Sexual Assault, Minnesota Department of Corrections, 1979.

Satir, V. *Conjoint family therapy.* Palo Alto, CA: Science and Behavior Books, 1967.

SEXUAL ABUSE
AND SEXUAL EDUCATION
IN CHILD-CARING INSTITUTIONS

David A. Shore, ACSW

"When he and Esther quarrelled, the crucial thing remained unspoken, leaving an atmosphere of wordless rancour and accusation" (Green, 1967, p. 23).

Over 400,000 children live in residential institutions such as treatment centers, temporary and long term shelters, detention homes, youth correctional facilities, centers for the mentally retarded and developmentally disabled, and group homes; at least an additional 400,000 live in foster homes (Harrell, & Orem, 1980). These children are largely voiceless and at the mercy of the adults who operate the institutions or agencies, as well as their fellow residents.

If one accepts the basic premise that the institutionalized are in many respects second class citizens, it is not surprising that we are first now turning our attention to institutionalized child abuse and neglect. Moreover, if a time line of our involvement with the problem of child abuse was plotted, it would be predictable that the sexual abuse of children in institutions would be to the far right of the time line. It might be suggested that child abuse "arrived" in the 1960's when Kempe and his colleagues at the Denver Medical Center introduced the diagnostic term "battered child syndrome" (Kempe, Silverman, Steele, Droegemueller & Silver 1962). The mid and late 1970s saw a dramatic increase in the attention we paid to one aspect of child abuse, the sexual abuse of children. One barometer of this is the increase in the number of articles appearing in the professional literature. In his review of fifty-six selected journals, Schlesinger (1981) found one hundred and seventeen articles on the sexual abuse of children between the years 1937–1980. Between 1937–1964 no more than one article was to appear in any given year. Between the years 1965–1974 the mean number of arti-

171

cles appearing was three with there being no more than four articles in any given year. For the years 1975–1980 the number of articles appearing was 9,4,13,22,22, and 15 respectively. It is interesting to note that while several articles where written on sex education in residential child-caring institutions during the years of Schlesingers' review, none were in the fifty-six periodicals representative of the helping professions. During this same forty-three year period the only articles to appear on sexual abuse in institutions dealt with the sexual abuse of juveniles in correctional settings (Shore, 1981).

It is hypothesized that, in part, the recent attention focused on institutional child abuse and neglect has developed out of the context of the increased concern for and study of familial child abuse and neglect. It is further suggested and hoped that this same process will now evolve into a greater involvement in one particular form of institutional child abuse and neglect—the sexual. There are many parallels and a number of important differences between maltreatment occurring within a child's own family and abuse or neglect occurring within a residential institution charged with the care of that child. There are types of abuse and neglect which are not only "institutional," that is, occurring in the context of an institution, but "institutionalized," as well. "Institutionalized" child abuse and neglect is that which is directly derivative from the nature of institutions, and, in most cases, at least tacitly supported by them (Harrell & Orem, 1980).

This article has four general purposes: (1) to explore the sexual neglect of children in institutions; (2) to explore the extent of sexual abuse of children in institutions; (3) to suggest that sexual neglect is a contributing factor to sexual abuse in institutions; and (4) to suggest some beginning solutions.

Expanding Parameters

When one reviews the literature on child sexual abuse, one finds a series of recurring themes. A thorough grounding of these myths and realities is presented throughout this volume and therefore will not be restated here, save for one—*sex begins at home.*

While the statement "sex begins at home" is well supported by the literature relative to the percentage of individuals who are sexually abused in some way before they reach the age of eighteen and often before they reach the steps outside their front door, the purpose of this paper is to expand the parameters of this now familiar statement to suggest that such abuse occurs (and perhaps more frequently) in the homelike institutional settings that "house" a significant percentage of the clients seen by social workers and other helping professionals.

While there is some solace to be gained in recognizing that sexual therapies, sexual education and sexual enrichment groups have gone a long way toward enhancing the sexuality of individuals and couples, unfortunately, until very recently, and with rare exception, these energies have been directed toward a sexually elite or *young, attractive, verbal,intelligent* and *successful* (YAVIS) population. The concept of "sexual trauma groups" should also go into our notion of expanding parameters.

Acknowledging that historically the needs of the YAVIS were of paramount concern puts us in a better position to now focus on the needs of non-YAVIS and sexually oppressed groups (Gochros, 1972, Shore, 1978; Shore, 1979). As this expansion process continues we must be aware of the fact that while techniques and curriculum established for and with YAVIS populations will be helpful, the overwhelming research indicates that such tools are not universally adaptable (Berelson & Steiner, 1964; White, 1956; Schofield, 1964; Goldstein, 1977; and Lorion, 1974). Therefore, clinical therapies and educational programs for sexual issues and problems, sex-related trauma, and sexual enrichment and enhancement groups must be developed and/or modified to meet the particular needs of *each* special population. Such techniques and curriculum are not, part and parcel, transferable.

As part of this continuing process, one group that is only now beginning to receive attention is the sexually abused and sexually neglected residing in child care institutions. Together these individuals constitute one of the largest of all special populations for whom social workers provide service. Despite this fact, with the exception of documented forced homosexual interactions in our prisons and jails, they remain one of the most invisible and oppressed of all our under-served populations—a population "at home" and behind closed doors. Included among these institutionalized groups are the mentally retarded, physically handicapped, mentally and medically ill, the dependent and neglected, the homeless and the imprisoned (See, Shore & Gochros, 1981).

More than two decades after Erving Goffman wrote *Asylums,* the definition of the *total institution* remains as salient as ever. "A total institution may be defined as a place of residence and work where a large number of like-situated individuals, cut off from the wider society for an appreciable period of time, together lead an enclosed, formally administered round of life" (Goffman, 1961, p. xii). By its very definition, the total institution attempts to manage all aspects of the lives of its inmates—including and especially their sexuality. As Neier points out, "privacy is not only unknown, it is the antithesis of life in a total institution" (Neier, 1978, p. 6). This, despite the fact that privacy is considered an intimately tied variable to developing a healthy sexuality. Such a premium is placed on privacy that standard 36.1 in the theraputic environment section of the *Consolidated Standards Manual for Child, Adolescent, and Adult Psychiatric, Alcoholism, and Drug Abuse Facilities* of the Joint Commission on Accreditation of Hospitals states, "The facility shall establish an environment that enhances the positive self-image of patients and preserves their human dignity." The chapter goes on to specify the term privacy in nine separate standards directly and eludes to it in several others, thereby making it the most prominent feature in the therapeutic environment chapter (JCAH, 1981).

While prisons serve as the proto—type of "the institution," we must appreciate that the prison environment is also found in institutions whose members have broken no laws. More than seven times the number of institutionalized are so confined, not for any wrongdoing, but because society believes confinement to be for their own good. Whether confinement is intended to be benevolent or punitive, institutions resemble each other in their treatment of inmates (Neier, 1978).

In our child-caring institutions, sexual activity, sexual acting out and sexual abuse are rampant. The consequences of such behavior are long term and contagious. Equally pervasive is the desire among residents for appropriate avenues of sexual expression and learning. A case in point was a study to determine the effects of institutionalization conducted in a long term residential facility for the physically handicapped in Toronto. The study reported the effects of institutionalization to be profound, long lasting and damaging to the individuals' ability to adjust to the world around them. As one of the few studies outside of a correctional facility to explore issues of human sexuality, sexual counseling was found to be missing from the program, despite the fact that all patients interviewed expressed a desire to make potentially sexual contacts with individuals who were not patients or staff at the facility (Carter, de Demeter, Fields, Jefferies, Warren, 1974).

Sexual Neglect

Descriptions and discussions of adolescence and more recently pre-adolescence almost invariably point to this group's need to establish appropriate sexual identities, concluding this task to be a major goal during this developmental phase. The role of parents in this phase-specific process is considered equally major (Lynn, 1962). Indeed, mention is frequently made of the potential difficulties in sexual identity resulting from disturbances in the parent-child relationship (Freud, 1958; Dignan, 1965; Benedek, 1959). Most notable among those who have pointed out the disastrous effects on infants brought up in institutionalized groups are Rene Spitz and John Bowlby. Spitz states that it is most damaging for any young child to be reared without benefit of a single "mother person" to take primary care of the child (Spitz, 1945; Spitz, 1946). Bowlby further concludes it to be critical to the mental health of the infant and young child that a warm, intimate, and continuous relationship with her or his "mother or permanent mother substitute" be experienced. Bowlby stressed three factors as especially pernicious to the child's mental health: first, no chance to form a close relationship to a "mother figure" during the first three years of life; second, maternal deprivation (separation trauma) for limited periods; and third, inconsistency, or changes from one mother figure to another during the first three years of life (Bowlby, 1951; Bowlby, 1958; Bowlby, 1960). While one may or may not choose to accept the analytical prerequisites established by Spitz, Bowlby and others, the impact of the institution as a mini-world is undeniable.

Perhaps it is this basic appreciation for the impact of the institution on a variety of aspects of sexuality that led the Child Welfare League of America, in its *CWLA Standards for Services of Child Welfare Institutions* (1964) to recommend that ". . . children (in foster care) should be given accurate and appropriate information about sex and should be helped to develop desirable attitudes and standards of sex behavior" (CWLA, 1964). Ironically, in its companion volume, *CWLA Standards for Family Care Services*, (1959) the only references to sexuality are that health services should include tests for venereal infections and that sleeping rooms should not be shared by children of the other sex.

It should not be surprising that the Child Welfare League of America does not, in any substantive fashion, address issues of human sexuality in institutions for dependent and neglected children. Other standard setting and accrediting bodies address this issue, if at all, in a passing fashion. In numerous ways, children's institutions are attempted microcosms of an intact family. Unfortunately, it is all too clear that a significant percentage of "intact families" avoid discussions of human sexuality, often leading to undesired or unplanned consequences. As we shall see, the institution exacerbates problem-causing issues in "intact families."

Despite sometimes our best efforts to the contrary, it is essential for the intact family as well as the "residential family" to recognize that either formally or informally, we are all in the business of teaching sexual education, sexual values and sexual expression. *There is no such thing as no sex education.* Information, attitudes and societal expectations are continuously being disseminated on both a conscious and unconscious level in the classroom, the dormitory or on the playground. By their very nature, residential facilities are placed in the position of having to provide numerous familial services concomitant with those we believe should be provided by the family. Among these services is sexual education and allowing for appropriate sexual expression.

It is hoped that these services are provided with the belief that it is the right of every individual to live in an environment of freely available information, knowledge, and wisdom about sexuality, so as to be enabled to realize his or her human potential. It is further recognized that sexuality is learned as the result of a process that should not be left to chance or ignorance. The definition of appropriate sexual expression will have to be carved out for each individual institution, as it is for every individual. One form of sexual expression considered acceptable by many facilities because of its limited individual and societial consequences is that of sexual self-pleasuring. Masturbation is today medically accepted as a natural and nonharmful part of sexual behavior for individuals of all ages and both sexes. It can help girls and boys to develop an affirmative sense of body autonomy. It can be a source of enjoyment and can provide an intense experience of the self as well as preparation for experiencing another. Equally important is the fact that many persons do not express their sexuality in this way and this also is an individual choice. While it is the role of each individual institution to decide the level of sex education it will provide and the kinds of sexual behavior it will condone, there is no debate about one form of sexual behavior considered unacceptable.

Sexual Abuse

The sexual victimization of juveniles in institutions other than correctional has received virtually no attention in the professional literature. By contrast the incidents of juvenile victimization abound in the criminology literature and will be cited here for its perspective. Fisher was the first to deal specifically with the issue of victimization, defining the term and developing various types of victimization that occurred in the institution under study (Fisher, 1961). Lockwood, in his study of prison sexual violence among men, defined five terms familiar to inmates and familiar, perhaps to a lesser degree, to residents of other types of juvenile facilities (Lockwood, 1980, p. 9).

—*Sexual Aggression:* behavior that leads a man to feel that he is the target of aggressive sexual intentions. The perception of the target becomes just as important as the objective actions of the aggressor in defining the situation. Sexual aggression can be viewed as a continuum marked by different levels of force. One end of the continuum might be a target imaging aggression from an aggressor's overture; the other end, the gang rape.

—*Aggressor:* the prisoner who initiates the incident.

—*Target:* the recipient of an approach perceived as aggressive. Some targets are victims of rapes; others flee when confronted with talk of sex. Most targets encounter some form of violence or verbal threat. Others, however, create a fearful situation from stimuli not definable as threatening by objective indices. (This author would consider all of these individuals "targets").

—*Sexual Assault:* forcible oral or anal sodomy.

—*Proposition:* request for sex that is not accompanied by force or threats.

Davis (1968, p. 9) raised disturbing questions about the extent to which juveniles were victims of stronger inmates in the Philadelphia Van System. In his study, he pointed out that inmates of all ages and degrees of criminality were stored together in vans awaiting disposition of their cases. The consequences of this were that younger boys had no chance, as older predatory males took advantage of them by beating and homosexually raping them, sometimes en masse. While the examples presented above reflect male institutions, variations of these themes are present in facilities for females.

Solutions to this problem are numerous and varied. The punitive ones are all too familiar. The less restrictive ones include privacy, which has already been cited, conjugal visitation and co-educational facilities. Less frequently mentioned, until quite recently, is the idea of providing sexual education for inmates and staff. The North Carolina Department of Corrections Pre-release and After-care Division has instituted a "Human Sexuality Day for Inmates" program. The one day a month program appears to be promising with its creators believing that as the day draws to a close each person has had several opportunities to deal with his own sexuality and to feel better about himself as a sexual person. Similar programs are under way or under consideration in other states. One suspects that the motivation for these programs may well have come from recent court decisions holding a sheriff or a municipal jail responsible for damages to a prisoner who is raped while in jail.

While the incidence of forced sexual behavior does not appear to be as prevalent in non-correctional facilities, the question nevertheless is raised, do the responsibilities of child welfare agencies for the total care and development of a child who is a temporary or permanent ward include a responsibility in the area of sex education? It is this author's experience that an increasing number of agencies throughout the United States and Canada are asking this question and concluding that in their role *in loco parentis*, the answer can only be yes.

Before actually discussing a sex education program as one component of combating sexual neglect and sexual abuse in child-caring facilities, an attempt will be made to link sexual education, sexual expression and sexual abuse.

Consequences of Deprivation of Body Pleasure

In Hannah Green's book, *I Never Promised You A Rose Garden*, (1967, p. 22), we read about Deborah's parents: "When he and Esther quarreled, the crucial things remained unspoken, leaving an atmosphere of wordless rancour and accusation." The guarded reference to the issues which are discussed in this paper results in a similar atmosphere in many residential establishments. Yet sexual education and sexual expression in residential institutions appear to be interacting forces that profoundly affect any institution—including sexual abuse. Prescott (1975, p. 11) elaborates the hypothesis that "deprivation of physical, sensory pleasure is the principal root cause of violence." This hypothesis, if valid, has far-reaching implications for our discussion, particularly with regard to our large institutions. A more extensive review of the literature cross referencing deprivation of body pleasure and the etiology of violent behavior suggests that violence has several causes and that early deprivation of pleasure has at least two major, opposing results: aggressiveness and withdrawal. Applying these consequences to sexual victimology translate to our earlier discussion of the *aggressor* and the *target*. We are also reminded that adolescence and pre-adolescence is often a time of sexual and emotional upheaval, and that the facilities that house these individuals present an equally emotionally and sexually charged atmosphere. Investigation into the interaction between emotional and sexual arousal has important implications for our discussion (Wolpe, 1978). Researchers and clinicians have generally assumed that anxiety and depression affect our sexuality (Masters & Johnson, 1970; Kaplan, 1974), and that anxiety reduction procedures, including education and outlets for expression, play a positive role in reducing sexual concerns. More recently, and more specifically, Wolchik and her colleagues (1980), in their laboratory study of the effects of emotional arousal on subsequent sexual arousal found that emotional reactions have a significant impact on sexual arousal. Mild anxiety facilitated sexual arousal; depression decreased sexual response.

It is this author's experience that sexual abuse and sexual confusion is alive and flourishing in a wide variety of institutions that house so many of our children.

Our challenge is to find an affirmative and positive way to integrate human sexuality with the whole of life.

Some Solutions

While child-caring institutions vary greatly in size, quality, reason for placement, and many other factors; they are bonded together by their responsibilities, and by their aspiration to provide for the fullest possible living experiences for the children assigned to their care. As has been suggested earlier in this article, a sex education program is considered one component of providing for the fullest possible living experience for the children assigned to institutions.

Sex Education Program—The task before those of us who work in child-caring facilities or who train individuals to work in such facilities, is to begin developing paradigms for such specialized needs. While such programs must be facility and population specific, much can be learned from the examples and experiences of existing sex education programs in residential child-caring facilities (Partak & Berner, 1977; Hausler & Scallon, 1977; Carrera & Juliana, 1977; Carrera & Baker, 1981). The desire of the facility should not be to reinvent the wheel. Moreover, one does not (successfully) develop a sexual education program in committee or purchase one from the outside and then implant it into a facility. Rather, it first and foremost requires the support and understanding of administration. Tied to this support will be legal and parental concerns that could ultimately have financial consequences because of a potentially "controversial program." Much homework is therefore required. An issue for all concerned—administration, parents, staff and residents—will be their own comfort and knowledge level with the subject matter. There should therefore be some instrument to evaluate this at the time of the proposal.

While emotions and defenses always run high when the subject is sex, the need for a slow, thought out systematic progressive-ratio-type approach to introducing a new program is by no means limited to the area of sexuality. During the past two years the author has had the opportunity to review newly implemented quality assurance programs in child, adolescent and adult psychiatric facilities throughout the United States. Those variables most tied to the successful implementation and integration of these programs included commitment from administration at the highest level, involvement of staff at the earliest stages and a willingness to move slowly in light of the impending resistance that always precedes and accompanies change. Returning to the area of sexuality, it is recommended that we encourage our students and staff to critically reflect and evaluate the ethical implications of such endeavors before embarking on a program (Johnson & Shore, 1982). We should also provide the necessary in-service training and classroom education that reflects a three component approach: cognitive, affective, and skills (Hallowitz & Shore, 1978).

While both the affective and skills components must be closely tied to such factors as the credentials of staff, funding sources, and the location of the facility, there is general agreement that the cognitive components should be comprised of three broad categories: (1) knowledge of sexual anatomy and physiology-related areas; (2) knowledge of psychosexual and psychosocial behavior; and (3) knowledge of sexual behavior and standards.

In concluding, we would do well to return to our beginning and recall our description of "institutional" and "institutionalized." As has been discussed, within the institution, aspects of life are institutionalized so as to cause or contribute to sexual neglect and/or abuse. As we look toward addressing this problem, it is suggested that we institutionalize factors that may lead toward a reduction of sexual neglect and abuse, if not an enhancement of one's sexual self. Such measures are needed to counterbalance measures taken to restrict the sexual growth and development of residents. In institutions, the repression of sexual activity is typically effectuated through sexual segregation of residents. This situation is then exacerbated by the fact that staff are usually assigned to work with residents of their own sex.

Most institutions have no guidelines covering allowable or prohibited sexual practice for residents (Mulhern, 1975). This leaves the determination of these guidelines largely at the discretion of staff. In an effort to reduce such subjective criteria, it is suggested that facilities establish ad hoc, interdisciplinary, sexual issues committees. Among the tasks of this committee should be the development of policies and procedures for addressing harmful sexual activities and a second set of policies and procedures for addressing training and program planning for appropriate sexual expression of residents.

Harmful Sexual Activities Policies and Procedures—such a document should be widely distributed and not remain within the hands of management personnel and in the rings of large three-ring binders exclusively. Since such a document may cause some anxiety among staff, it should begin with a reasonable introduction that might include the following:

> It is a continuing responsibility of all staff to do all that is possible to prevent harmful sexual activities. When such nonetheless occur, it is the staff's continuing responsibility to respond actively and definitively to protect children from further harm and to help them deal with the impact of whatever has taken place.

Remember that the failure of care-taking adults to take explicit action after an overt event often implies active condoning of the action in the minds of children. After an introduction setting the tone for the policy and its rationale, the policy should provide a specific framework for preventive and responsive staff action to control and remedy sexually harmful activities by and affecting children in the facility. If this is the first explicit enunciation of such policies, let staff know that said policies will be amended as experience in implementing these ideas accumulates. Invite staff input and solicit their feedback while showing them that perhaps unlike certain other policies and procedures, this one will be a living document. Among the topics that should be considered for inclusion in policies and procedures are sexual abuse between residents and sexual contact between staff and residents. The former should include such areas as prevention, education, staff responses to harmful sexual activities (with definitions and basic principles of response) and factors affecting intervention, to name but a few. The set of guidelines for sexual contact between staff and residents should be equally as proscriptive, discriminating between physical and sexual contact along with examples of each and outlining the consequences of actions that do not conform to the policies and procedures.

Training and Program Planning Policies and Procedures—a second task of the ad hoc committee might be to draft guidelines for training and program planning for appropriate sexual expression of residents. Here the statement of purpose can be quite simple; for example, "To apply the principle of normalization of training and program planning for residents and to provide training for program staff to assist residents in their sociosexual development according to their individual needs." The policy then might simply state that "the facility shall provide or obtain training for residents that ad-

dresses the development of age-appropriate sociosexual behavior."
It is at this point that you might find the services of an outside
consultant of some value. Such policies and procedures might go on
to suggest target groups (for example, all residents, all staff, applicable service providers, parents, guardians). It should also include a
set of standards and procedures. This then might be your beginning.

It is hoped that this article will serve you well both as a point of
discussion among students and staff and as a starting point by staff.
Remember, there is no time to lose. During the time it took to read
this brief article, your residents have already started!

REFERENCES

Benedek, T. Sexual functions in women and their disturbances. In S. Arieti (Ed.),
American Handbook of Psychiatry, 1959, 1, 727–748.
Berelson, B. & Steiner, G.A. *Human Behavior: An inventory of scientific findings.*
New York: Harcourt Brace and World, 1964.
Bowlby, J. Maternal care and mental health. Geneva: *World Health Organization
Monograph.* 1951.
Bowlby, J. The nature of the child's tie to his mother. *International Journal of
Psycho-Analysis,* 1958, 39, 350–373.
Bowlby, J. Separation anxiety. *International Journal of Psycho-Analysis,* 1960, 41,
89–111.
Carrera, M.A. & Juliana, J. A human sexuality program in a residential treatment
center. *Child Care Quarterly,* 1977, 6, 222–230.
Carrera, M.A. & Baker, E.A. A human sexuality program that worked. In L.
Brown, (Ed.) *Sex education in the eighties.* New York: Plenum Press, 1981, 145–
162.
Carter, C., de Demeter, D., Fields, L., Jefferies, A & Warren, W. The impact of
institutionalization. *Dimensions of Health Services.* 1974, 43.
Child Welfare League of America. *CWLA standards for family foster care services.*
New York: Child Welfare League of America, 1959.
Child Welfare League of America. *CWLA standards for services of child welfare
institutions.* New York: Child Welfare League of America, 1964.
Davis, A.J. Sexual assault in the Philadelphia prison system and sheriff's van. *Trans-
action.* 1968, 12, 8–16.
Dignan, M.H. Ego identity and maternal identification. *Journal of Personality and
Social Psychology,* 1965, 1, 476–486.
Fisher, S. Social organization in a correctional residence. *Pacific Sociological Review.*
1961, 4, 87–93.
Freud, A. Adolescence. In R. Eissler, et al. (Eds.) *The Psychoanalytic Study of the
Child.* New York: International Universities Press, 1958, 13, 255–278.
Gochros, H. L. The sexually oppressed. *Social Work.* 1972, 17, 16–23.
Goffman, E. *Asylums: essays on the social situation of mental patients and other
inmates.* Garden City, New York: Archor Books, 1961.
Goldstein, A.P. *Structured learning therapy: toward a psychotherapy for the poor.*
New York: Academic Press, 1973.
Green, H. *I never promised you a rose garden.* London: Pan Books, 1967.

Hallowitz, E. & Shore, D.A. Small group process in teaching human sexuality. *Health and Social Work,* 1978, 3, 132–151.
Harrell, S. & Orem, R. *Preventing child abuse and neglect: a guide for staff in residential institutions.* Washington, D.C.: U.S. Department of Health and Human Services, 1980.
Hausler, R. & Scallon, R.J. Sex education in a residential child caring agency. *Child Care Quarterly,* 1977, 6, 211–221.
Johnson, J. & Shore, D.A. Teaching human sexuality and social work values. *Health and Social Work,* 1982, 7, 41–49.
Joint Commission on Accreditation of Hospitals. *Consolidated standards manual for child, adolescent, and adult psychiatric, alcoholism, and drug abuse facilities.* Chicago: JCAH, 1981, 149–153.
Kaplan, H.S. *The new sex therapy.* New York: Brunner/Mazel, 1974.
Kempe, C.H., Silverman, F.N., Steele, B.F., Droegemueller, W. & Silver, H.K. The battered child syndrome. *Journal of the American Medical Association.* 1962, 181, 17–24.
Lockwood, D. *Prison sexual violence.* New York: Elsevier North Holland, 1980.
Lorion, R.P. Socioeconomic status and traditional treatment approaches reconsidered. *Psychological Bulletin.* 1974, 79, 263–270.
Lynn, D.B. Sex role and parental identification. *Child Development.* 1962, 33, 555–564.
Masters, W.H. & Johnson, V.E. *Human sexual inadequacy.* Boston: Little, Brown, 1970.
Mulhern, T.J. Survey of reported sexual behavior and policies characterizing residential facilities for retarded citizens. *American Journal of Mental Deficiency.* 1975, 79, 679–673.
Neier, A. Sex and confinement. *The Civil Liberties Review.* 1978, 5, 6–16.
Partak, L. & Berner, G.P. Sex education and the behavior problem child. *Child Care Quarterly,* 1977, 6, 204–210.
Prescott, J.W. Body pleasure and the origins of violence. *Bulletin of the Atomic Scientists,* 1975, 31, 10–20.
Schlesinger, B. *Sexual abuse of children: an annotated bibliography—1937–1980.* Toronto: University of Toronto Press, 1981.
Schofield, W. *Psychotherapy: the purchase of friendship.* Englewood Cliffs, New Jersey: Prentice-Hall, 1964.
Shore, D.A. Special populations: the next sexual frontier. *Journal of Sex Education and Therapy.* 1978, 4, 35–36.
Shore, D.A. Handicappism and the non-YAVIS. *British Journal of Sexual Medicine.* 1979, 6, 23–24.
Shore, D.A. *Sex-related issues in correctional facilities.* Chicago: The Playboy Foundation, 1981.
Shore, D.A. & Gochros, H.L. *Sexual problems of adolescents in institutions.* Springfield, Illinois: Charles C. Thomas, 1981.
Spitz, R. Hospitalism: an inquiry into the genesis of psychiatric conditions in early childhood. In, *The Psychoanalytic Study of the Child.* New York: International Universities Press, 1945, 1, 53–74.
Spitz, R. Hospitalism: a follow-up report. In, *The Psychoanalytic Study of the Child.* New York: International Universities Press, 1946, 2, 113–117.
White, R.W. *The abnormal personality.* New York: The Ronald Press, 1956.
Wolchik, S.A., Beggs, V.E., Wincze, J.P., Sakheim, D.K., Barlow, D.H. & Mavis-sakalian, M. The effect of emotional arousal on subsequent sexual arousal in men. *Journal of Abnormal Psychology,* 1980, 89, 595–598.
Wolpe, J. Comment on "A test of reciprocal inhibition" by Hoon, Wincze, and Hoon. *Journal of Abnormal Psychology,* 1978, 87, 452–454.